Shaken & Stirred

Tim Brown

Written by
Jake La Rue

A *Delilah* BOOK

DISTRIBUTED BY
THE PUTNAM PUBLISHING GROUP
NEW   YORK

A Delilah Book
Delilah Communications, Ltd.
118 East 25th Street
New York, N.Y. 10010

ISBN: 0-88715-003-9

First published in the United States of America
by Delilah Communications, Ltd. in 1984

Originally published in the United Kingdom
by Paper Tiger Books Dragon's World Ltd in 1983.

Design and execution of all photographs by
TIM BROWN

Photographed exclusively on Mamiya RZ67
Models from Sarah Cape Model Agency
Cocktail accessories courtesy of The Cocktail Shop,
5 Avery Row London W.1
Specialised retouching by Carlton Fox Ltd

Designed by Steve Henderson

Printed in Singapore

Contents

Introduction

"Candy is dandy," observed the American poet Ogden Nash, "but liquor is quicker." Nash was surely reflecting, in his own inimitable way, on the subtle and persuasive effects of the great American cocktail, for ever since Eve's apple fermented, alcohol, in some form or another has been employed to breach maidenly defences and inflame latent desire. As the old saying goes: "Little drops of whisky, little drops of gin, makes a lady wonder where on earth she's bin."

Alcohol, it has been claimed, is not an aphrodisiac (though some people make a special case for green chartreuse) but it swiftly side-steps inhibitions and unlocks certain doors. The psychologist Havelock Ellis recommended alcohol **in small quantities** as a beneficial aid to sexual performance—too much has the opposite effect—but that depends on how much you need to get you going.

Early cookery books—and particularly French ones—included recipes for such exotic stimulants as "Huile de Venus", a combination of eau de vie (brandy), sugar, spices, the aromatic gum benzoin, infused almond leaves and a pinch of saffron to impart a golden hue. The result you either drank or rubbed lovingly into your partner's body—perhaps both.

Some drinks are known for their rapid action, sherry for example, while others are known for their effects. Champagne, unlike most things in life, actually lives up to its faintly wicked reputation as a loosener of tongues and it was thus the natural choice to accompany the notorious **petit soupers** served in the elegant brothels of 18th century France. The Marquis de Sade (who also had a reputation to uphold) declared that one should serve burgundy with the hors d'oeuvres, bordeaux with the entrée and champagne with the roast, followed by tokay and madeira (popular passion-stirrers of the period) with the

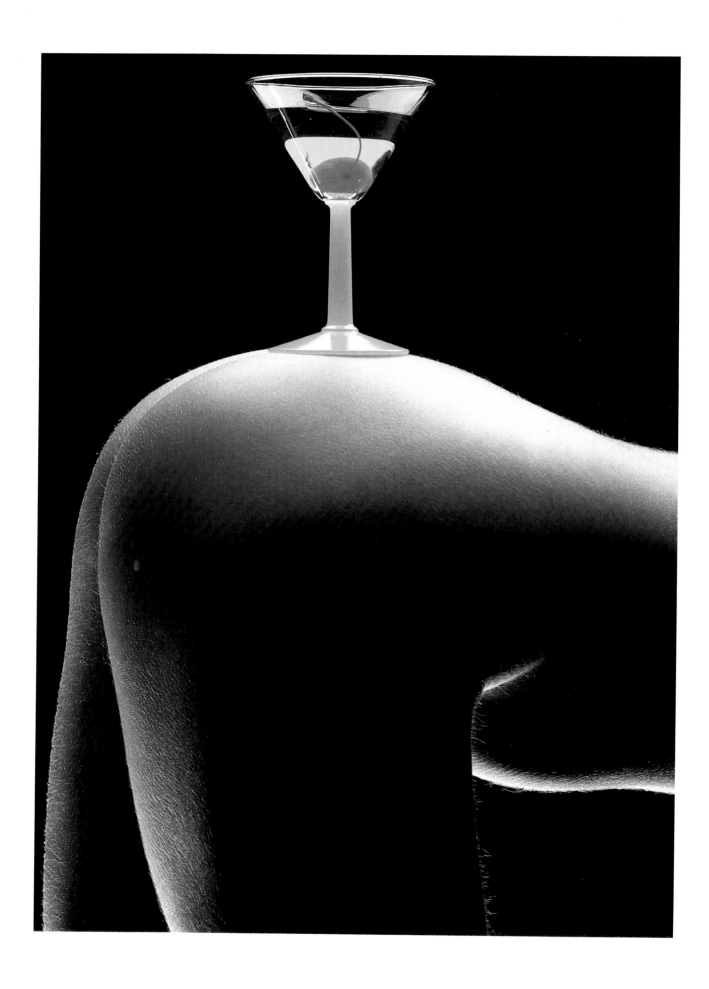

dessert, while Madame de Pompadour (who ought to know) said that "Champagne is the only wine that leaves a woman beautiful after drinking it."

In cocktails, gin is certainly the most popular and "feminine" spirit, and a typically alluring cocktail might be the **Bijou**, being three parts gin, one part green chartreuse and one part Italian vermouth—and you know what Italians are! Add a dash of orange bitters and shake with ice.

The enticing character of most liqueurs comes from spices or herbs, and spice is the base of many perfumes. The legendary hedonist Norman Douglas in his book **Venus in the Kitchen** includes several aphrodisiac drinks, such as this one featuring nutmeg, a known opiate: "two lumps of sugar and eight drops of curaçao. Fill up the glass with port. Put it in a receptacle and boil it. Take it off the fire and serve it with a slice of lemon and nutmeg sprinkled over it." Douglas also includes an "After-Love Drink", the creamy texture of which illustrates another seductive property often exploited in a cocktail. This was made with madeira wine plus "a quarter glass of maraschino, a whole egg yolk unbroken, a measure of cream, a quarter glass of brandy" to be swallowed in one gulp! Whether or not Douglas knew it, this drink is a version of the cocktail called **Knickebein**—or maybe it should be Knickerbein …

A cocktail, then, shaken or stirred, and poured into glasses for two to share, must be strong enough to excite the senses, just sweet enough to hint at sensuality, and a pleasure to the eye and ear—the tinkle of ice, the soft plop of an olive or grape, the rhythm of the shaker, the swoosh of soda, all serve to accelerate the pleasure and quicken the pulse. The effect of a cocktail, properly made, is as well attested today as when these lines were written, more than two hundred years ago:

From thee [alcohol], my Chloe's
    radiant eye,

New sparkling beams receives;
Her cheeks imbibe a rosier dye;
Her beauteous bosom heaves.

Summon'd to love by thy alarms,
Oh with what nervous heat!
Worthy the Fair, we fill their arms,
And oft our bliss repeat.

All we can add to that noble sentiment is "Bottoms Up!"

Fundamentals

What is a cocktail? Take the classic **Martini** for example. This is the archetypal cocktail for, in the mid-nineteenth century, a "cocktail" was a combination of gin (specifically a type known as "Old Tom"), dry vermouth and orange bitters, shaken with ice—in other words, a **Martini**. The versatility of gin as a base spirit has led to its use in at least 150 different cocktails, and it has been suggested that cocktails were devised purely to mask the harsh taste of poor-quality gin. A more likely explanation, however, is that mixed drinks are simply the result of man's inventiveness and constant search for novelty. Indeed, it is variety that is the only true aphrodisiac …

What constitutes a particular cocktail varies from barman to barman, and from book to book—and there have been many books on the art of mixed drinking, from **The Old Waldorf-Astoria Bar Book** and **The Savoy Cocktail Book** to David Embury's excellent guide, **The Fine Art Of Mixing Drinks**.

Cocktails can be strong, like the **Torpedo**; seductive, like the **Pink Lady**; shattering, like the **Thunderclap**; sensual, like **Between The Sheets**; swinging, like the **Tango**; even sentimental, like the **Last Kiss**.

The variations are endless: substitute or omit an ingredient and you end up with a different drink altogether. For example, **Damn The Weather** (orange juice, Italian vermouth, gin and curaçao) also pours under the name of either **Will Rogers** or **Cloudy With Showers**, depending on which cocktail book you have to hand. If you leave out the vermouth, however, you have a **Hula-Hula**, also known as a **Hawaiian**; omit the curaçao and you have the **Abbey cocktail**. Switch French vermouth for the curaçao and your drink is now a **Chorus Girl**. If you don't have any curaçao but there's a bottle of peach brandy lurking at the back of the cupboard (you should be so lucky), mix it with your gin, vermouth and orange juice and you have a **Peter Pan**. Omit the orange juice and it's a **Snyder**. You don't have sweet vermouth, only dry? Never mind, you do have a **Tango**. So however limited the ingredients, you can still have a choice to offer your expectant guests.

In cocktail recipes the ingredients are usually measured in parts—2 parts gin to 1 part such and such—for as much as the ingredients themselves may change, it is their proportions that dictates the drink. A typical **Martini** consists (or should consist) of 6 to 7 parts gin to 1 part dry vermouth. Equal parts gin and vermouth will give you a **Gin And It**, while a ratio of 17 parts gin to 1 of vermouth results in what is sometimes known as **Death In The Afternoon** (or any other time of day, for that matter). So how much liquid is a part? The answer seems to be more a question of interpretation than fluid ounces. If you measured your 6 parts gin and 1 part vermouth using an egg-cup your guest would be prostrate—and not quite in the manner you had in mind. To avoid messing about with teaspoons, the best thing is to approximate the quantities. Use your eye. It's what professional barmen do. In fact, they measure by **time**—at the barmen's school long hours are spent pouring liquid from a bottle into a measure until they can learn how long it takes to pour, say, one-third of a gill of a specific liquor. To save you wearing out your stopwatch we would make the following suggestion. When making a cocktail, say a **Side Car**, judge how much liquor would be

needed to fill the glass. A standard cocktail glass holds between 3 and 4 fluid ounces, so you would need half a glass of brandy (approx 2 fluid ounces) and top up with half and half lemon juice and Cointreau (a scant fluid ounce of each). The ultimate criterion of course, is taste.

Should a cocktail be shaken or stirred? Upon this weighty question much has been written and spilled. The **Savoy Cocktail** book has this to say on the subject: "Since the **Savoy Book** first appeared [about 1930] there has been a change in the practise of cocktail mixing. Then it was considered correct to shake most cocktails. Now it is regarded as incorrect to do this, unless there is a fruit juice or wine base. Stir a clear mixture, shake a cloudy one."

Experts (except perhaps for James Bond) prefer their **Martini** stirred, knowing that a shaken **Martini** is weaker on account of the ice packed in the shaker. Furthermore, a shaken **Martini**, containing as it does a wine-based ingredient (the vermouth) will lose its transluscence. However, shaking makes for a much colder drink, and a good cocktail must be stimulatingly cold to the point of brief and pleasurable anaesthesia. The moral seems to be: chill your glasses in the refrigerator and stir in the bar glass or shaker with plenty of ice. Barmen use a heavy beer-type glass with a silver container that fits over the rim and real ice—not those cubes like kiddies' bricks.

For bar equipment, apart from the standard cocktail glasses, you will need tall, straight-sided glasses (such as those sold as Collins, Highball or Zombie glasses) for long drinks with carbonated waters or fruit juice, Old Fashioned glasses (chunky Scotch tumblers with a thick base), and goblets on a stem . A long-handled mixing spoon for stirring is vital, as are a strainer and a sharp knife for paring fruit peel. Also useful is sugar syrup, which you make by boiling equal parts sugar and water (i.e. half a pound to half a pint) for about two minutes. Store in a bottle in the fridge.

FINE CHAMPAGNE
COGNAC

Duty Free

A nice way of picking something up before taking off.

Shirley Temple

A good way to cool down, apart from taking a cold shower, is to sip a tall glass of ginger ale, with a dash of grenadine, over ice cubes.

Shirley Jane, however, is Shirley Temple's naughty sister. She holds onto the grenadine but replaces the ginger ale with as much rye whisky as she dares—plus a spoonful of sugar to make the medicine go down.

Mack The Knife

Commonly known as the **Bartender**, this is the sort of cocktail that goes for the throat or at best stretches you out on the floor. We have included it to show the desperate measures to which some barmen are driven in order to find a new way of dislocating the nervous system. The cocktail (it's a cocktail?) comprises equal parts of gin, dry sherry, French vermouth and Dubonnet, with a dash of curaçao or Grand Marnier for seasoning. It is a variation on the classic **Baron**, but with the addition of sherry, and Dubonnet in place of sweet vermouth.

Golden Screw

This was invented in the days when a screw was something that held two planks together, being an **Orange Blossom** made with vodka instead of gin:

1 part vodka
3 parts orange juice

The modern version, however, goes as follows:

1 part Drambuie
1 part Lemon Hart rum
1 part dry sherry

Stir with ice in a bar glass, strain into cocktail glasses, and drop a delicate spiral of lemon peel into each. The blonde is optional.

Shorts

The advantage of shorts, or briefs if you prefer, is that they are easy to take—or rather put—down. A short drink is simply a quick one: scotch on the rocks, pink gin, **Martini** or any other mixture which bypasses such frills as fruit juice, egg white, coconut cream or anything else that would get in the way of the alcohol. **Highballs** are liquor based drinks topped up with a carbonated beverage, like a gin and tonic or a whisky and ginger ale, but they are not short, or even low. **Slings** and **daisies** are not short, nor are **fixes** and **rickeys**, **bucks** and **collinses**. Delicious though they may be, all these go for the slow burn … Let's hear it for the short, sharp shock!

Banana Bliss

A simple brandy cocktail, related to the
Stinger (see page 55), Banana Bliss
comprises equal parts of crème de banane
and brandy. If this is too sweet for your taste,
increase the brandy and add a dash of
Angostura bitters. Shake with ice and strain
into a cocktail glass. Drink slowly, while
peeling off.

Chocolate Soldier

2 parts Dubonnet
4 parts gin
1 part lime juice

Moist, brown and clinging, this cocktail is improved if served in the bed in preference to on the rocks. Pour the ingredients into a shaker with ice. Turn down the lights, turn up the music, and shake to a fast beat.

Scotch On The Rocks

Scotsmen usually prefer to pursue their pleasures in comfort as having it on the rocks is wet and windy. This is known in America as coming through the rye.

Dizzy Dame

Not so much from the high life as the effect on the more responsive areas of the body of this concoction:

   1 part brandy
   1 part kahlua or Tia Maria
   dash cherry brandy
   1 part cream

Shake together with ice, pour into a goblet and, as a precaution, administer while horizontal.

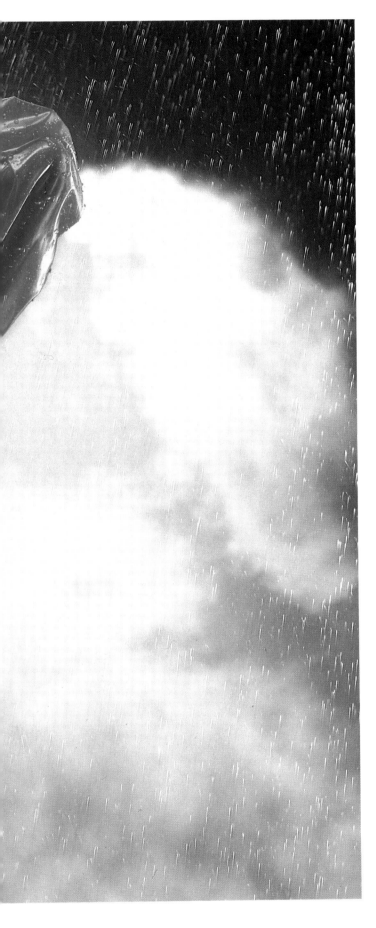

Whisky Mac

This is perhaps the only true Hibernian cocktail. Admittedly the **Bobby Burns** (equal parts whisky and Drambuie), has its adherents as does this recently unearthed 19th century recipe:

½ gill whisky
1 teaspoon bitters
2 drops essence of cinnamon
sugar syrup to sweeten
½lb ice, pounded

The Whisky Mac itself is a cold-weather drink for when there's a nip in the air and you prefer staying in bed. It is made as follows:

2 parts Scotch whisky
1 part ginger wine

Some people add a dash of hot water.

Dry Martini

For many, the ultimate cocktail, and companion to the **Manhattan**. Historians of the cocktail tell us that the Martini was originally called the **Martinez** and was made with sweet, Italian vermouth instead of the usual dry, French vermouth. There are no strict rules for making a Martini cocktail, since tastes vary, but the general guidelines are as follows: use the best quality gin and a good French vermouth such as Noilly Prat (dry sherry is an excellent substitute) in the ratio of 1 part vermouth to 6 or 7 parts gin. Equal parts of gin and vermouth is not recognised as a Martini but simply as a **Gin And French**. Some cocktail fanciers keep their gin in the refrigerator, and add the vermouth with an eye dropper, or merely pass the vermouth cork over the glass. We do not advocate such mean measures. If you want a Martini **that** dry, use an umbrella ...

The cocktail should be refreshingly frosty but never frigid, and stirred, not shaken. Why? Because shaking dilutes the alcohol more than if you stir it with ice in a suitable container, and shaking may rob the Martini of its characteristic, crystalline translucence and create a cloudy appearance. (David Embury, ultimate authority on the Martini, says that if you shake a Martini instead of stirring it, the drink is known as a **Bradford**.) A twist of lemon peel over the surface, and the addition of a green olive completes the picture—a masterpiece. In New York city, where the Martini is held in the highest esteem, drinkers sometimes refuse the olive, commanding the barman to "hold the fruit", since they maintain the olive displaces the liquor, lowers the temperature, and soaks up some of the precious liquid. The more brusque, hard-edged customers may be heard to snarl, "When I want a fruit salad I'll ask for it."

A cocktail pearl onion in place of the olive produces a **Gibson** cocktail.

The Rose

1 part dry vermouth
1 part grenadine, cherry brandy or something equally pink
4 parts gin

Pour into a mixing glass, add ice and stir in a provocative fashion. The Rose turns pink those parts which other cocktails cannot reach ...

Page 34

Bloody Mary

Before, during or the morning after, this versatile mixture would soften even the stony heart of the Queen whose name it bears:

> 1 part vodka
> 4 parts tomato juice
> couple of dashes Worcestershire sauce
> dash lemon juice
> pinch celery salt
> salt and pepper to taste

Substitute beef bouillon or condensed consommé for the tomato juice and you have a **Bullshot**, half and half and it's a **Bloodshot** (which is probably how you'll feel when you wish you hadn't).

Golden Slipper

The classic recipe for this drink calls for a measure of yellow chartreuse to be poured into a **pousse café** glass (or any tall, straight-sided glass on a stem) followed by an egg yolk (broken) floated on top and finally a measure of Danzig Goldwasser, poured over the back of a teaspoon. It was a drink specially created for the **poule de luxe,** the girl who has everything—and more where that came from.

Pousse cafés (literally: to push coffee down) are made up of liqueurs selected for their colour and different densities, poured by turn (heaviest first) so that they remain in layers, an operation for which you need patience and a steady hand. For a drink destined for the bedroom, however, when you can't rely on a steady anything, try this variation: equal parts yellow chartreuse and either apricot or peach brandy, thoroughly shaken with ice. The result will be divinely sweet, as smooth as a silk stocking and guaranteed to make her toes curl.

Midnight

This is the drink to have ready when both hands are pointing upwards; it will keep them occupied for a breathing space:

> 2 demi-tasse cups of black coffee
> 1 measure Tia Maria
> Whipped cream

Pour the liqueur into the coffee and float the whipped cream on top. (Is this a Cuban or Jamaican coffee?)

Mixing

The one-handed horizontal shake, as well as giving the practitioner a new angle on things, will ensure that they mix in the most interesting circles (not to mention up and down!)

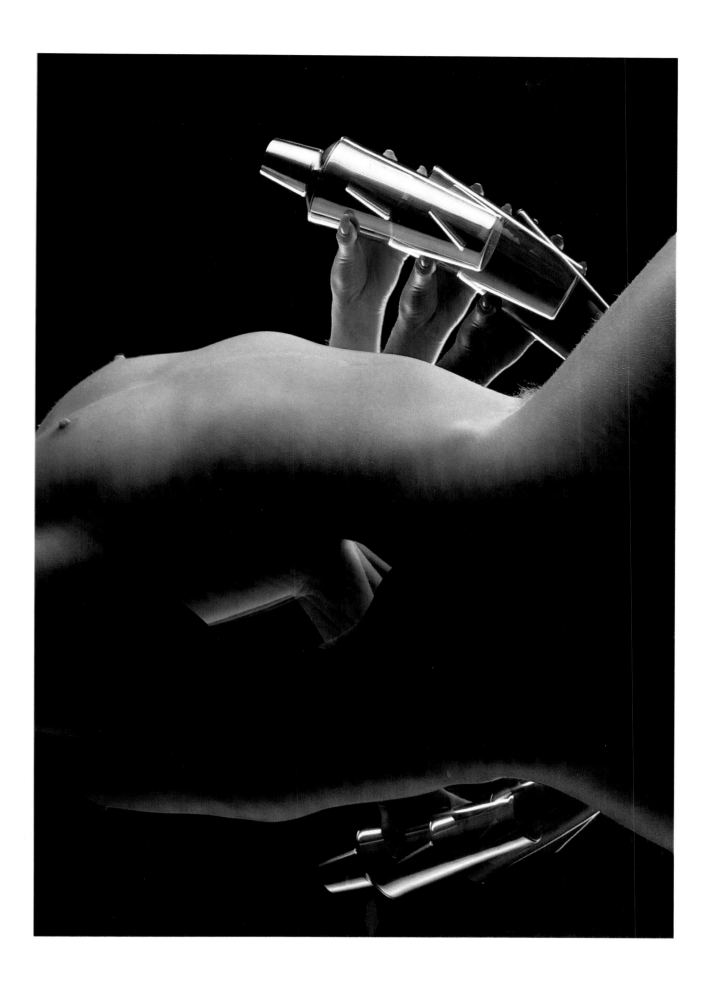

Night Light

For those who prefer not to feel their way in the dark we recommend the following:

   2 parts white rum
   1 part orange curaçao
   1 egg yolk for each two drinks

Shake ingredients well with ice, and strain into goblets.

Black Velvet

Pour equal parts of champagne and Guinness stout simultaneously into a tall glass with a steady hand. Called variously **Champagne Velvet**, **Velvet**, or sometimes **Bismarck**, the combination results in a very black, very smooth and satiny drink with a concealed effervescence that imparts a tingling sensation to the tongue, and elsewhere. It is also an ideal drink for the "morning after".

Mix-Up

Being the polite name for any cocktail that involves an inordinate number of ingredients. A fine example is the **Almagoozlum** which might, in wine circles, be considered as made from bin ends:

> 1 part Holland Gin
> 4 parts water
> 3 parts sugar syrup
> 3 parts yellow chartreuse
> 3 parts Jamaica rum
> 1 egg white for each two drinks
> 1 part curaçao
> 1 part bitters

Shake with crushed ice, strain into chilled glasses, light the blue touch-paper and stand well back!

Silk Stockings

Basically an **Alexander**, with tequila instead of the gin, this cocktail is more in the nature of a dessert than a drink and may be best tackled with a spoon:

> 4 parts tequila
> 2 parts white crème de menthe
> dash of grenadine
> generous measure cream

Put all ingredients into a blender with lots of ice. Turn it on full speed ahead and when nicely mixed and frothy, pour into glasses. Sprinkle with a little cinnamon and garnish with a garter.

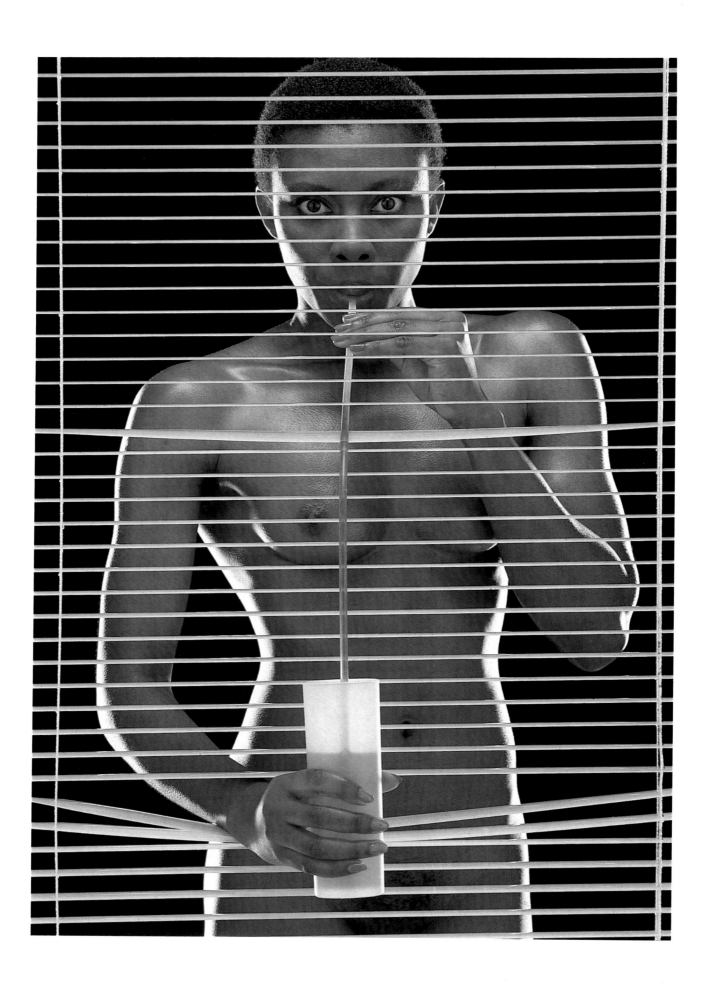

Venetian Sling

2 parts gin
1 part Campari
1 part Galliano

Stir, pour over ice and top up with soda. Also known in some circles as **Blind Man's Buff**, this variation on the classic **Singapore Sling** might not get you as far as the mysterious East, but you'll be floating down the Grand Canal in no time.

Fun In Bed

    1 part brandy
    1 part grape juice

Shaken with ice, this might not be quite what the Little Fellow had in mind but Good-Time Charlie would certainly approve.

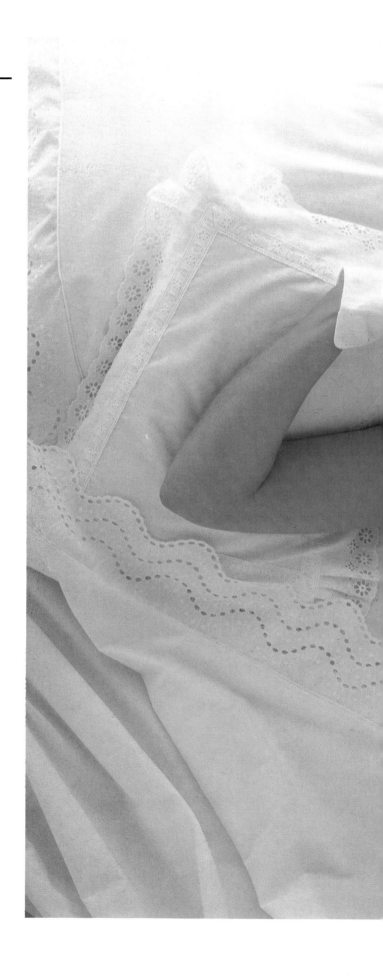

Pink Pussy

2 parts Campari
1 part peach brandy
1 egg white to every two drinks

Put all the ingredients into a shaker with ice.
Agitate until well blended, thick and creamy,
and eject into chilled glasses.

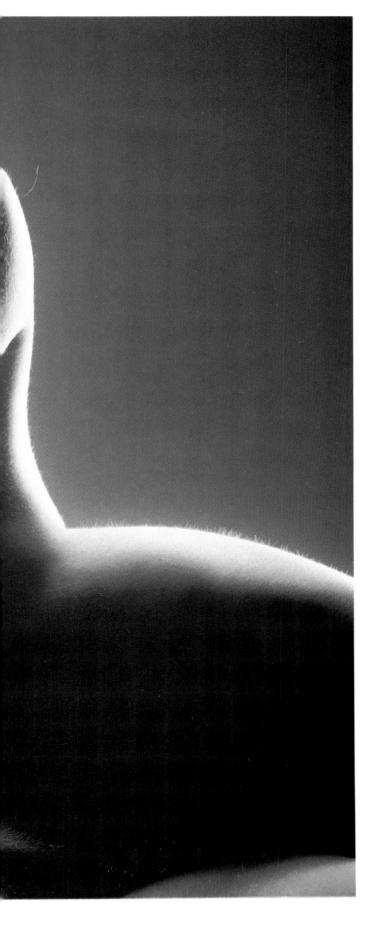

Brandy

Brandy, and someone to share it with, is better suited to Intermission than Overture. Those who like their brandy au naturel might be interested to know that after many years of exhaustive (and exhausting) research, experts have finally concluded that the perfect receptacle for this most aromatic of spirits is the human navel. Unbreakable, unspillable (if kept firmly in the horizontal position) and with a built-in warming device, it might not hold as much as the conventional brandy glass, but it makes drinking much more fun.

More energetic readers might care to try their brandy chilled; as a **Stinger**, for example:

2 parts brandy
1 part white crème de menthe

Stir with cracked ice and serve either straight or on the rocks.

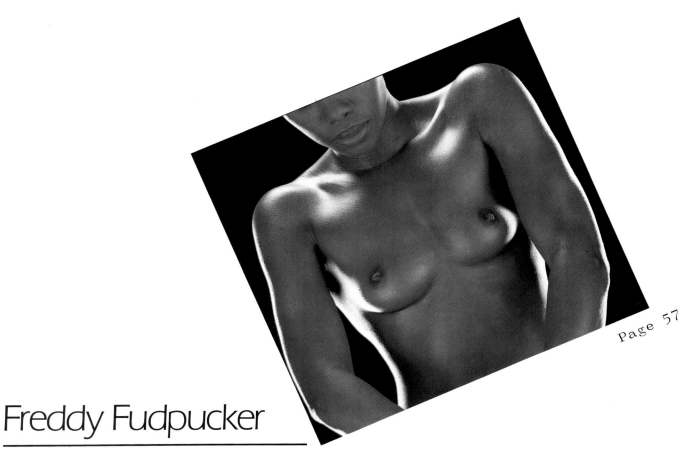

Freddy Fudpucker

Tequilla, the basis of this drink, is by no means everybody's cup of tea, and the practise of drinking it with salt and a squeeze of lemon juice is simply to disguise the flavour of the crude spirit.

Another way to do this is to dilute it with orange juice and sweeten with a liqueur, such as the newly-arrived Galliano, used in the **Harvey Wallbanger**. Harvey's lesser known cousin, Freddy Fudpucker, is constructed from the following:

    1 part tequilla
    orange juice
    1 part Galliano

Shake well with ice, and serve with a straw or two.

Fudpucker is, of course, the anagram of Duckprufe.

58

Blue Lagoon

1 part blue curaçao
1 part vodka
lemonade

This may have been named after the popular novel (later the subject of two movies) by De Vere Stacpoole about a boy and girl shipwrecked on a desert island who grow to adulthood without the benefit of sex education.

Curaçao is an orange-based liqueur from the Dutch West Indies, so the Blue Lagoon theme is appropriate, but for a more tropical effect we suggest you try replacing the vodka with white rum, such as Bacardi. Serve it on the rocks, with plenty of ice.

If you omit the lemonade and present the drink in a cocktail glass, you have a **Blue Monday**.

Bamboo

This is a wine-based and non-spiritous (though not entirely spiritless—both vermouth and sherry are fortified wines) cocktail, also known as **Amour**, which, as every schoolboy knows, is French. The **Old Waldorf-Astoria Bar Book** lists this cocktail as the **Armour**. So, if either amour, or even armour (though chain mail is more flexible) is what you need, then stir together the following:

1 part dry sherry
1 part French vermouth
dash of orange bitters

Pour over ice cubes and serve with a twist of lemon. Replace the dry vermouth with sweet and you have an **Adonis**.

What is done with the bamboo is, of course, up to you ...

Pink Lady

1 part grenadine
2 parts lemon juice
2 parts applejack brandy
5 parts gin
1 egg white to each two drinks

Shake all together with ice, strain into cocktail glasses, and if she doesn't turn pink, she's no lady.

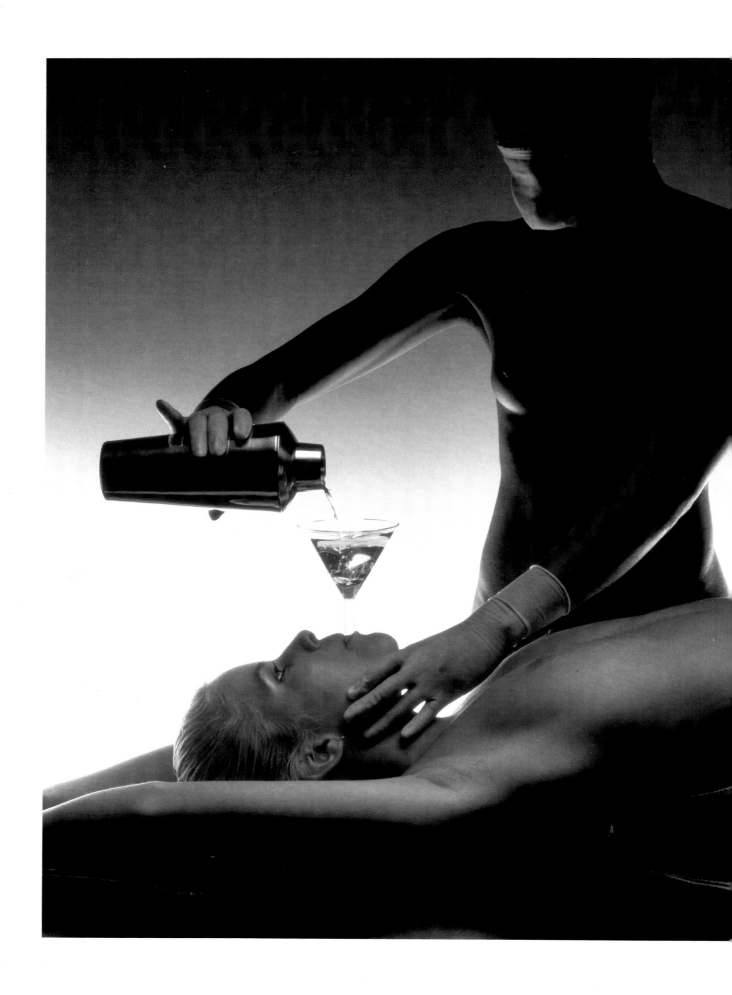

Black Mischief

1 part grape juice
1 part Mandarine Napoléon
(tangerine liqueur)

Mix and top up with chilled, sparkling white wine. Drop one black grape into the glass, split another and balance it on the rim.

Between The Sheets

1 part Cointreau
2 parts lime juice
3 parts brandy
3 parts rum

Shake all together with crushed ice. Add a twist of lemon peel if desired. Enough said.

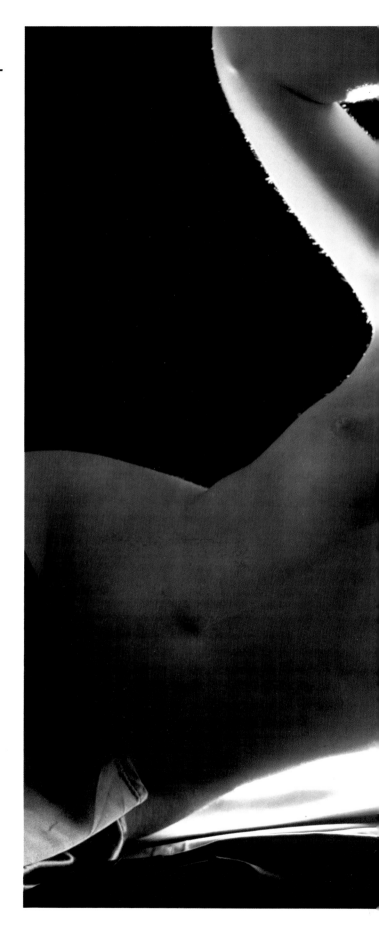

Blue Lady

Based on the famous **White Lady**, invented in Paris at the start of the 1920s, itself a variation on the basic **Gin Sour**, the thoroughly modern Blue Lady uses blue curaçao instead of Cointreau as follows:

> 1 part fresh lemon juice
> 2 parts blue curaçao
> 7 to 8 parts gin
> 1 egg white to each two drinks

Shake all ingredients passionately with ice until creamy and cold, but not frigid. A blue lady could do with warming up, but if the above should fail to ignite her, there are other ways ...

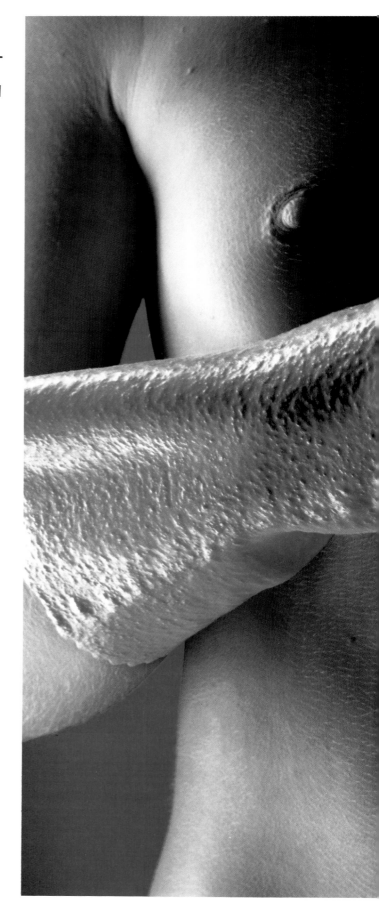

Damn The Weather

(A drink to rekindle interest in old flames.)

> 1 part orange juice
> 1 part Italian vermouth
> 5 parts gin
> 3 dashes orange curaçao

Shake the above vigorously with ice, strain into a goblet and decorate with slices of orange and a cherry. The orange juice refreshes, the dry vermouth balances the sweetness of the fruit and the curaçao, and the gin holds it all together.

The fireside, by the way, has long been associated with feminine warmth and fecundity, especially in ancient Rome, where the goddess Fornax ruled the hearth. A **fornax** was a hearth or oven—a **fornix** was a brothel.

Refreshers

Tall, long, cool drinks, usually with a carbonated beverage, refresh, revive and rejuvenate, so that you can, in effect, take up again more or less where you left off.

*A **Highball** is any spirit diluted with a fizzy partner, such as Scotch and soda or gin and tonic, or the famous **Horse's Neck**: your choice of spirit in a tall glass, filled up with ginger ale, ice and a spiral of lemon peel draped over the edge of the glass—on the inside, of course.*

*A **Buck** is gin, ginger ale and lemon juice with ice.*

*A **Rickey** is a choice of spirit with fresh lime juice, plus sugar syrup and a sweet liqueur.*

*A **Collins** is a tall drink of spirit—such as gin—with lemon juice, sugar syrup, soda water and ice.*

*A **Fizz** is made with the same ingredients as a **Collins**, but should be very well iced, and charged with very fizzy, foaming soda water.*

Corpse Reviver

Supposedly a means of bringing the dead (drunk?) back to life or, alternatively, delivering the **coup de grace**, the following may have been what Dr Frankenstein used:

1 part arrack or Swedish Punch (a blend of rum and aquavit)
1 part Cointreau
3 parts gin
1 part Pernod
1 part lemon juice

Shake until you peacefully expire.
A gentler reviver is this recipe:

1 part brandy
4 parts milk
dash of Angostura bitters
sugar to sweeten

Pour into a goblet, stir and top up with soda water. Once there is a sign of life, help her back to bed.

Up In Mabel's Room

1 part grapefruit juice
1 part golden, runny honey
2 parts bourbon whisky

Mabel was the extremely accommodating barmaid at New York's Hartford hotel during the 1940s. Her instructions were to "shake with cracked ice, strain into a cocktail glass, decorate with a cherry and a grapefruit segment, and take it lying down."

Fallen Angel

This variation on the **Gin Sour**, minus the bitters, is also known as a **Greenback**:

7 parts gin
2 parts green crème de menthe
juice of a lemon or lime
dash of Angostura bitters

Shake well with ice and strain into cocktail glasses, and add to each a green maraschino cherry. This drink's distinctly greenish tinge is in deference to the envy of all those who wish they'd fallen too.

Index

Manufactured in Singapore

EXECUTIVE EDITOR
Natalie Earnheart

CREATIVE TEAM
Jenny Doan, Natalie Earnheart, Christine Ricks,
Tyler MacBeth, Mike Brunner, Lauren Dorton,
Jennifer Dowling, Dustin Weant, Jessica Toye,
Kimberly Forman, Denise Lane

EDITORS & COPYWRITERS
Nichole Spravzoff, Camille Maddox,
David Litherland, Julie Barber-Arutyunyan

SEWIST TEAM
Jenny Doan, Natalie Earnheart, Carol Henderson,
Janice Richardson, Aislinn Earnheart

PRINTING COORDINATOR
Rob Stoebener

PRINTING SERVICES
Walsworth Print Group
803 South Missouri
Marceline, MO 64658

LOCATIONS
Fran Esry Home, Hamilton, MO
Kauffman Center for the Performing Arts,
    Kansas City, MO
The Nelson-Atkins Museum of Art, Kansas City, MO
Christopher S. Bond Bridge, Kansas City, MO
Kansas City River Market, Kansas City, MO

CONTACT US
Missouri Star Quilt Company
114 N Davis
Hamilton, MO 64644
888-571-1122
info@missouriquiltco.com

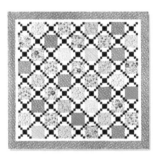

contents

Oops! Sometimes we make mistakes. To find corrections to every issue of BLOCK go to: **www.msqc.co/corrections**

3

A note from Jenny

Home is Where the Quilts Are

Dear Quilters,

Writing to you from the comfort of home is a privilege in this fast-paced world. I often find myself between places, driving long distances or flying to far-off locations to visit quilters around the world. It can be hard to feel comfortable in such circumstances, but I've found out something incredible about the quilting world. No matter where I go, as long as I can find a quilt shop, I feel right at home. After all, home is where the quilts are!

Home is such a lovely place to be. I've recently dug into my sewing studio for a bit of spring cleaning and I've unearthed some truly vintage finds! It's been a pleasure to sort through my treasured fabric stash again and remember what I really love about quilting—the feel of the fabric, the joy of selecting a stack of prints and sewing them together without a pattern. Cutting, stitching, pressing, and repeating the process over and over. There's something very comforting about it and I look forward to spending time with these simple creative pursuits whenever I get a spare moment.

This spring, let's dig into quilting with renewed vitality! Do what is necessary to start fresh, whether it's a bit of light cleaning and dusting or a major fabric stash overhaul, and you'll be amazed to find yourself itching to get back behind a sewing machine again. Celebrate the art of quilting by treating your machine, your fabrics, and your space with gratitude and you'll be rewarded every time.

Jenny

JENNY DOAN
MISSOURI STAR QUILT CO.

Try Our App

It's easy to keep up on every issue of BLOCK magazine. Access it from all your devices. And when you subscribe to BLOCK, it's free with your subscription! For the app, search BLOCK magazine in the app store. Available for both Apple and Android.

Missouri Bicentennial Quilt

"I hope that viewers of the quilt will spend time learning new things about their fellow Missourians and make connections across differences."

Michael Sweeney
Bicentennial Coordinator

Throughout the past 200 years, quilts have been an unmistakable part of Missouri's heritage. From the early pioneer days to modern times, quilting remains a part of the culture, style, and tradition of this great state. As a way of commemorating Missouri's Bicentennial, the State Historical Society of Missouri and Missouri Star Quilt Co., in partnership with the Missouri State Quilters Guild, have teamed up to create the Missouri Bicentennial Quilt! It includes one quilt block from each and every county as well as the independent City of St. Louis, to create a quilt showcasing the unique characteristics of Missouri culture and important moments in Missouri's history. We had a moment to speak with Michael Sweeney, the Bicentennial Coordinator, and he shared a glimpse into the process of bringing this beautiful quilt to life. Let's take a closer look!

Livingston 1837

MFA Founded
March 10, 1914

COUNTY
SEAT
PARIS,
MO.

FOUNDED - 1837

8

What sparked the idea for this quilt?

"There were actually a couple of 'threads' that came together to inspire the project. Quilting has been and remains a fundamental part of the creative and social life of many people in the State of Missouri. I'm particularly fascinated by the social aspect, seeing quilting as a shared activity, done in groups as part of quilting circles or guilds or as a tradition. So, recognizing the centrality of quilting in the lives of many Missourians, using quilts and quilting in some facet of the Missouri Bicentennial commemoration just made sense."

"Missouri is a pretty provincial place. Everybody is sort of doing their own thing. It's really hard to put your finger on symbols and ideas that all Missourians share. So, one of the overarching aims of the Missouri Bicentennial Commemoration has been to provide folks across the state the opportunity to articulate aspects of their unique communities, counties, and regions with the goal—not of coming to a single statement about who all Missourians are—but rather coming to a sense of 'shared something-ness,' as recognition of something shared across difference. And the Missouri Bicentennial Quilt is one project that pushes towards that goal."

"The final outcome of the quilt is a set of incredibly diverse blocks that are all, in one way or another, creative expressions of place, showcasing the diversity of place in Missouri while bringing those individual expressions into a shared view. I hope that viewers of the quilt will spend time learning new things about their fellow Missourians and making connections across differences."

Who is responsible for bringing this quilt to life?

"In 2013, the State Historical Society of Missouri was asked by the 97th Missouri General Assembly to develop a plan to celebrate the Missouri Bicentennial and one of those projects was the Missouri Bicentennial Quilt."

"Missouri Star generously offered to donate labor and materials to assemble the quilt and provide further direction to the project. I do not have to tell you that Missouri Star is a fantastic Missouri success story, a valuable member of the Hamilton community, and well-respected across the state and beyond. They were an ideal partner, and I am tremendously grateful the company agreed to participate in this once-in-a-generation project. Courtenay Hughes and Mary Bonnette, in particular, shepherded the project at Missouri Star. I cannot say enough wonderful things about these two and their commitment to seeing the Missouri Bicentennial Quilt to completion."

"Quilting has been and remains a fundamental part of the creative and social life of many people in the State of Missouri."

"We received a total of 203 submissions from 173 contributors. From these contributions, one block was selected to represent each county in the state."

How did you accomplish this great task?

"With lots and lots of help! Quilt block submissions were accepted from October 8, 2018, through September 2, 2019. After assistance from Missouri State Quilters Guild and Courtenay's husband Bob Hughes, we received a total of 203 submissions from 173 contributors. From these contributions, one block was selected to represent each county in the state as well as the independent City of St. Louis. In addition to these 115 blocks, there are a few special blocks in the final quilt representing each of the partners: The State Historical Society of Missouri, Missouri Star Quilt Co., the Missouri State Quilters Guild, the Missouri Governor's Mansion, and the Missouri Division of Tourism."

What are some notable events depicted on the quilt?

"I'm not even sure where to start! People, including Ella Ewing, Calamity Jane, Dale Carnegie, George Washington Carver. Architectural features, including the Locust Creek Bridge, Harry Truman birthplace, Newcomer School, the Y-Bridge, county courthouses, Grant's Farm. Historical events, including the Honey War, westward expansion, Osage Trail, and more. There is a lot here!"

What do you hope for people to take away from their experience viewing the quilt?

"I hope people walk away with a greater sense of—and appreciation for—the state's tremendous geographic and cultural diversity while identifying points of connection within that diversity. Again, this whole notion of getting to know your fellow Missourians. The better we know each other, the better we'll be at solving common problems."

The Bicentennial Quilt will travel on throughout the state. The quilt will also be displayed at the Statehood Day events in Jefferson City in August 2021 and at the 2021 Missouri State Fair. Be sure to come see it during Missouri Star's Birthday Bash this September 2020!

When the Missouri Bicentennial Quilt is done with its year-long journey, it will remain with the State Historical Society of Missouri as part of its permanent collection, available to been seen and enjoyed for hopefully another 200 years!

"... this notion of getting to know your fellow Missourians. The better we know each other, the better we'll be at solving common problems."

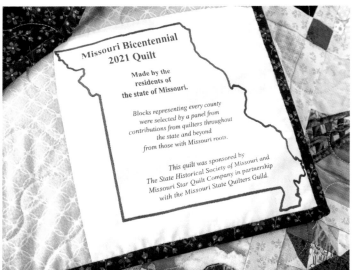

Missouri Bicentennial
2021 Quilt

Made by the
residents of
the state of Missouri.

Blocks representing every county
were selected by a panel from
contributions from quilters throughout
the state and beyond
from those with Missouri roots.

This quilt was sponsored by
The State Historical Society of Missouri and
Missouri Star Quilt Company in partnership
with the Missouri State Quilters Guild.

For the tutorial and everything
you need to make this quilt visit
www.msqc.co/BlockV7issue2

Ruby Sensation Sew-Along

PART 1

Ravishing in red, the Ruby Sensation sew-along is a brand new addition to BLOCK we think you'll adore! For four more issues, you can follow along and create this gorgeous quilt one section at a time. It's made up entirely of crimson-hued fabrics with a crisp, white background, but you can make it in any colors or prints you can imagine. It could easily be made to look more traditional or more modern and we can't wait to see what you'll come up with.

Each quilt block has been chosen carefully to create a pattern that is totally unique. Nothing like it has been made before! We've included favorites like the Missouri Star block, the 54-40 or Fight block, the Sidekick block, and more, to combine into an eye-catching design. For the rest of this year, you'll build your own beautiful quilt, one section at a time with each new issue of BLOCK.

It all begins with the center star, a radiant version of the classic Missouri Star. Sew along with us and you'll be guided through the whole process, from start to finish. We think you'll be amazed at what you can do! Keep on stitching and by the end, you'll have your very own Ruby Sensation quilt to get cozy with. Let's get started!

FULL QUILT

MATERIALS

QUILT SIZE
86" x 86"

QUILT TOP
1¼ yards fabric A
1¼ yards fabric B
1½ yards fabric C
1¼ yards fabric D
5½ yards background fabric
 - includes inner border

OUTER BORDER
1½ yards

BINDING
¾ yard

BACKING
6¼ yards – vertical seam(s)
 or 2½ yards 108" wide

SAMPLE QUILT
Kona Solids Crimson, Chinese Red, Tomato, Sienna, White

FABRIC KEY

A - Crimson

B - Chinese Red

C - Tomato

D - Sienna

MISSOURI STAR (Block Only)

MATERIALS

BLOCK SIZE
24½" unfinished, 24" finished

BLOCK
¼ yard fabric A or (1) 10" square
¼ yard fabric B or (2) 10" squares
¼ yard fabric C or (2) 10" squares
1 yard background fabric or (9) 10" squares

1 cut

Note: This quilt is precut friendly! If you'd like to sew along using 10″ squares instead of the yardage we have shown, skip the fabric cutting directions below. Trim the 10″ B and C fabric squares to 7½″. From the 10″ background squares, trim 4 squares to 7″ and 4 squares to 6½″.

From fabric A, cut:
- (1) 10″ strip across the width of the fabric. Subcut (1) 10″ square.

From fabrics B and C, cut:
- (1) 7½″ strip across the width of the fabric. Subcut into (2) 7½″ squares.

Set the remaining strip pieces of fabric A, fabric B and fabric C aside with the rest of the remaining fabric.

From the background fabric, cut:
- (1) 10″ strip subcut across the width of the fabric. Subcut (1) 10″ square. Trim the remaining strip to 7″ and subcut into (4) 7″ squares.
- (1) 6½″ strip across the width of the fabric. Subcut into (4) 6½″ squares.

2 make center half-square triangles

Layer the 10″ background square on top of the 10″ fabric A square and sew around the perimeter of the squares ¼″ from the edge. Cut from corner to corner twice on the diagonal. Press open and square units to 6½″ for a **total of 4** center half-square triangle units. Set aside for the moment. **2A**

3 make star leg units

Draw a line from corner to corner once on the diagonal on the reverse side of both of the 7½″ fabric C squares. Layer a marked 7½″ fabric C square with a 7½″ fabric B square. Sew on both sides of the drawn line using a ¼″ seam allowance. Cut on the drawn line to reveal 2 half-square triangles. Open and press the seam allowance toward the darker fabric. **Make 4** B/C half-square triangle units. **3A**

Draw a line from corner to corner once on the diagonal on the reverse side of the 7″ background squares. Layer a marked background square with a B/C half-square triangle, making sure that the drawn line crosses over the seam on the half-square triangle. Sew on both sides of the drawn line using a ¼″ seam allowance. Cut on the drawn line. Open to reveal 2 star leg units and press the seam allowance to 1 side. Square to 6½″. **Make 8**. **3B**

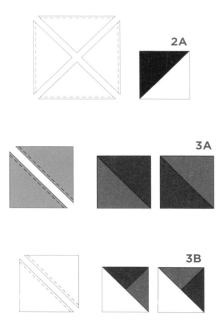

2A

3A

3B

4 block construction

For the first and fourth rows of the block, sew (2) 6½" background squares and 2 star leg units together, as shown. **Make 2**. **4A**

For the second and third rows, sew 2 star leg units and 2 center half-square triangles together, as shown. **Make 2**. **4B**

Refer to the diagram to your right to layout the block. Press the seams of the first and third rows to the right. Press the seams of the second and fourth rows to the left. Nest the seams and sew the rows together to complete our first block of this lovely quilt—the Missouri Star Block!

Block Size: 24½" unfinished, 24" finished

4A

4B

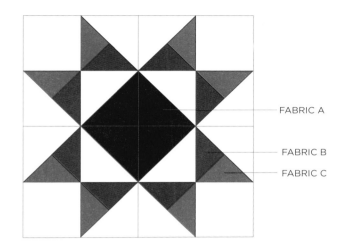

FABRIC A

FABRIC B

FABRIC C

15

Without pause, without a doubt, in a heartbeat. I'll keep choosing you.

For the tutorial and everything you need to make this quilt visit: www.msqc.co/BlockV7issue2

An Ode to Quilting
Irish Change Quilt

What does a quilt mean to you? To many of us, a quilt is more than a blanket to keep us warm at night, something that can add color to a drab living room, or a project to pass the time. Quilts mean so much to us because they're a way for us to tell stories and to preserve our most precious memories. If you think about it, quilts are like colorful extensions of ourselves. If this sounds right to you, then you might really resonate with these lovely poems about quilts and quilting.

Quilt Poem
by Sandra Stanutz

This quilt has rules as you will see
They are for you to follow as dictated by me

This quilt must be used in some manner or way
You can throw it on the floor, you have my okay

If you are chilly, use it to warm up
Or throw it in your truck or give it to a pup

Use it on a table, have a picnic or two
Give it to the needy the choice is up to you

The worst thing you could do that would make me quite sad
Is to put it away and say, "Best quilt I ever had."

This quilt is given to you as a way to say I care
So find a use for it soon, that is my dare!

The Quilting
by Linda McGee Huntington

The aunts, thimble in hand and children in tow
Each took her place around the broad expanse
Of yet unstitched quilt.

A labor of love this quilting.
Bits of Grandpa's shirt
Scraps from Lucy's Easter dress.

One by one with dolls and tea sets
We slipped beneath the quilt
To play and listen.

"What silly old women," we thought,
As they laughed and cried
And stitched memories.

If anyone can write something so sweet and heartwarming about a quilt, it just proves that these soft works of heart really are much more than blankets. From start to finish, there's a story or memory behind each stitch and square, and it's important to preserve those stories and memories because they are what make us love and treasure quilts the way we do.

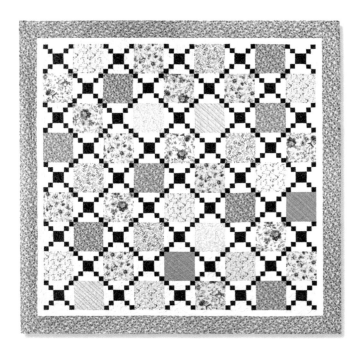

materials

QUILT SIZE
100½" x 100½"

BLOCK SIZE
10" unfinished, 9½" finished

QUILT TOP
1 package 10" print squares
1½ yards accent fabric
3¼ yards background fabric
  – includes inner border

OUTER BORDER
1¾ yards

BINDING
1 yard

BACKING
9¼ yards – vertical seam(s)
  or 3¼ yards 108" wide

SAMPLE QUILT
Sketchbook Garden by Lisa Audit for
Wilmington Prints
Bella Solids - American Blue by Moda Fabrics

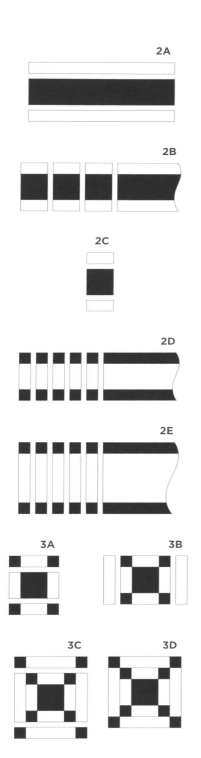

1 cut

From the accent fabric, cut:
- (16) 2″ strips across the width of the fabric.
- (5) 4″ strips across the width of the fabric. From 1 strip, subcut (1) 4″ square and set the remainder of the strip aside for another project.

From the background fabric, cut:
- (8) 2″ strips across the width of the fabric.
- (4) 4″ strips across the width of the fabric. Subcut (1) 4″ x 2″ rectangle from each of 2 strips.
- (8) 7″ strips across the width of the fabric. Subcut 4 strips into 7″ x 2″ rectangles. A **total of (82)** 7″ x 2″ background rectangles are needed.

2 make units

A units

Using a ¼″ seam allowance, sew a 2″ background strip to the top and bottom of a 4″ accent strip. Press the seams toward the center. **Make 4. 2A**

Cut each of these strip sets into (10) 4″ increments to create A units. **2B**

Sew a 4″ x 2″ background rectangle to the top and bottom of the 4″ accent square to create 1 additional A unit for a **total of 41**. Press the seams towards the accent fabric. **2C**

B units

Sew a 2″ accent strip to the top and bottom of a 4″ background strip. Press the seams toward the accent fabric. **Make 4.**

Cut each of these strip sets into (21) 2″ increments to create a **total of 82** B units. **2D**

C units

Sew a 2″ accent strip to the top and bottom of a 7″ background strip. Press the seams toward the background fabric. **Make 4.**

Cut each of these strip sets into (21) 2″ increments to create a **total of 82** C units. **2E**

3 block construction

Lay 1 A unit and 2 B units in 3 rows as shown. Nest the seams and sew the rows together to complete the block center. **3A**

Sew a 7″ x 2″ background rectangle to either side of the block center. Press the seams toward the outside edges. **3B**

Sew a C unit to the top and bottom of the center unit, nesting the seams as you go. Repeat the previous instructions above to **make 41** blocks. Press. **3C 3D**

Block Size: 10″ unfinished, 9½″ finished

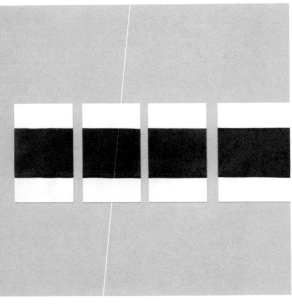

1   Sew a 2" background strip to the top and bottom of a 4" accent strip. Press the seams toward the center. Make 4. Cut each of these strip sets into (10) 4" increments to create A units.

2   Sew a 2" accent strip to the top and bottom of a 4" background strip. Press the seams toward the accent fabric. Make 4. Cut each of these strip sets into (21) 2" increments to create a total of 82 B units.

3   Sew a 2" accent strip to the top and bottom of a 7" background strip. Press the seams toward the background fabric. Make 4. Cut each of these strip sets into (21) 2" increments to create a total of 82 C units.

4   Lay 1 A unit and 2 B units in 3 rows as shown. Nest the seams and sew the rows together to complete the block center.

5   Sew a 7" x 2" background rectangle to either side of the block center. Press the seams toward the outside edges.

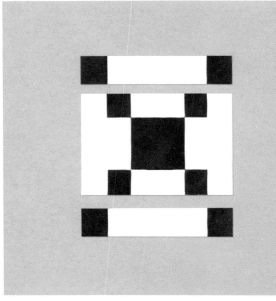

6   Sew a C unit to the top and bottom of the center unit, nesting the seams as you go. Repeat the previous instructions above to make 41 blocks. Press.

4 arrange & sew

Referring to the diagram below, lay out your blocks and 10" print squares in **9 rows of 9**, alternating your pieced blocks with print squares. Each odd row will begin with a pieced block and each even row will begin with a print square. Sew the blocks together in rows. Press the seam allowances of all odd-numbered rows to the left and all even-numbered rows to the right. Nest the seams and sew the rows together to complete the quilt center.

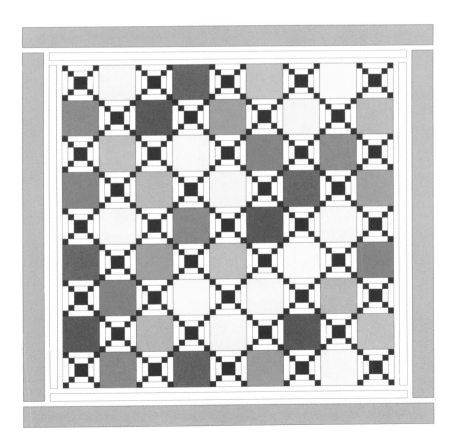

5 inner border

Cut (9) 2½" strips across the width of the fabric. Sew the strips together end-to-end to make 1 long strip. Trim the inner borders from this strip.

Refer to Borders (pg. 102) in the Construction Basics to measure and cut the inner borders. The strips are approximately 86" for the sides and approximately 90" for the top and bottom.

6 outer border

Cut (10) 6" strips across the width of the fabric. Sew the strips together end-to-end to make 1 long strip. Trim the outer borders from this strip.

Refer to Borders (pg. 102) in the Construction Basics to measure and cut the outer borders. The strips are approximately 90" for the sides and approximately 101" for the top and bottom.

7 quilt & bind

Layer the quilt with batting and backing and quilt. After the quilting is complete, square up the quilt and trim away all excess batting and backing. Add binding to complete the quilt. See Construction Basics (pg. 102) for binding instructions.

Hello again!

Here you'll find my latest personal quilting projects. I'm so excited I get to share them with you! You all know that I work hard every week to help create brand new quilting tutorials, and I absolutely love it, but it's also nice to take a break and make something for the sheer joy of it. These personal projects are my little way of relaxing. You never know what you'll find here, so stay tuned and you'll be surprised every issue!

Jenny

Learn more about fussy cutting on pg. 38. This easy cutting technique really takes quilt blocks to the next level!

Mini Pincushion
Designed by Laura Heine
Made by Jenny Doan
Finished Fall 2019

The humble tomato pincushion doesn't get much fanfare, but it is a staple in the sewing room! Every time I go to Quilt Market, I'm inspired by the beautiful quilts I see and this sweet wall hanging featuring a beautifully pieced tomato pincushion stole my heart. I knew I had to make it to hang in my sewing studio!

I am intrigued by the collage piecing method used in this project. When we had a "Laura Heine certified" teacher come to town to teach a class, I felt compelled to take the class and learn it myself. The teacher was amazing and so encouraging. She even rounded up a group of helpers to iron and cut with me. I had so much fun learning this method! It really taught me to look at fabrics differently. I love how we can take little bits and pieces of fabric and put them together to create something amazing.

Tiny House Quilt
(appears on left page)
Made by Jenny Doan
Finished Winter 2018

House quilts are so classic and completely adorable. Each little house block has its own unique personality and, in my mind, a different little family that lives inside! Creating a quilt like this was an absolute pleasure and I looked forward to piecing little houses each day. Now I have my very own Tiny House quilt hanging in my home and it's become one of my all-time favorite quilts!

Over the years, I kept seeing many versions of these adorable tiny house quilts popping up online and I wanted to come up with a really easy way to make them using precut fabrics. It only takes two charm packs and it comes out so cute. I did some experimenting and once I got started, I couldn't stop! At first, I was making one a day as a practice, but then I couldn't wait any longer to see the quilt finished. I spent an entire weekend making the rest of the blocks. As an added bonus, I had so much fun fussy cutting little characters for the doors and the bright colors just make it so happy. You can make your own when you follow along with Misty and me on YouTube. Be sure to share it at **#msqcshowandtell**. I can't wait to see what you do with it!

For the tutorial and everything you need to make this quilt visit www.msqc.co/BlockV7issue2

A Quilt's Life
Luminary Quilt

I remember the last binding stitch, whipped into place by skilled hands. She paused for a moment, let out a contented sigh, and let her hands glide over my fine piecing. I was the twelfth quilt completed that year, the fifty-seventh since she had started counting in 1945. Who knows how many came before that?

Over the years Anne had quilted for her children and grandchildren. She had quilted for friends and neighbors. She had donated hand-stitched quilts to fund-raising events, homeless shelters, and the maternity ward of St. Mary's.

Even so, I couldn't help but think that I was special. Pieced with love and quilted by hand, I was to be a wedding gift for a very special great-granddaughter.

After being carefully inspected for stray pins and hanging threads, I was wrapped in white tissue paper and a shining teal ribbon and presented to young Melanie and her handsome groom.

Life with the newlyweds was grand. I had a place of prominence on an always-neat bed. Clean, tidy, peaceful. Then came the baby.

I quickly became acquainted with long, sleepless nights. But that wasn't the worst of it! Little Charlie wasn't just an insomniac, he was a huge mess maker, too! Spit up and leaky diapers were soon followed by crayon scribbles and sticky fingers. My once-crisp piecing grew soft and worn. Countless visits to the washing machine muted my colors and frayed my binding. I lost my spot of prominence on the bed and began a second life as a picnic quilt.

I gotta tell ya, I was a little apprehensive at first, but it turns out life in the car is grand! I've been to baseball games and firework shows. I've seen half a dozen movies at the drive-in theater. I've gone camping in the woods, for goodness sake!

And when little Charlie went away to college, was it a flawlessly new quilt he wanted to take with? No sir! It was me! After all, I've been there since the day he was born. I smell like home. I'm filled with memories. I represent comfort.

Yes, it's been a fine life, and though I look a bit worse for the wear, I wouldn't trade a single moment. A well-worn quilt is a happy quilt!

materials

QUILT SIZE
58" x 72"

BLOCK SIZE
12½" unfinished, 12" finished

QUILT TOP
3 packages 5" print squares
  - includes cornerstones
3¾ yards background fabric
  - includes sashing

BINDING
¾ yard

BACKING
3¾ yards - horizontal seam(s)

SAMPLE QUILT
Good Times by American Jane for
Moda Fabrics

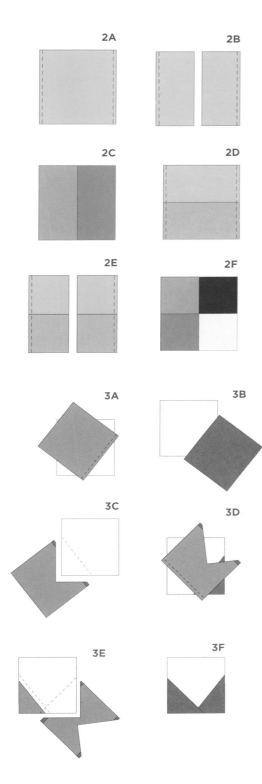

2A 2B

2C 2D

2E 2F

3A 3B

3C 3D

3E 3F

1 sort & cut

From the background fabric, cut (18) 4½" strips across the width of the fabric. Subcut (9) 4½" squares from each strip for a **total of (160)** 4½" background squares. Set the background squares aside for now.

Select (80) 5" print squares and set them aside for the star legs.

Select (8) 5" print squares and cut each in half vertically and horizontally to create (4) 2½" squares from each. Set 30 of these 2½" print squares aside for your cornerstones.

2 make 4-patches

Select (20) 5" print squares for your 4-patch star centers. Set the rest of the 5" print squares aside for another project.

Layer a 5" print square atop a differing 5" print square right sides together. Sew down the 2 sides of the square with a ¼" seam allowance. **2A**

Cut the sewn squares in half vertically. **2B**

Open to reveal 2 strip units. Repeat pairing, sewing, and cutting the remaining 5" print squares you selected. Press the seam allowances of each strip unit toward the darker fabric. **2C**

Select 2 differing strip units. With seams running horizontally and right sides together, layer 1 unit on top of the other. Sew down the 2 sides of the strip units using a ¼" seam allowance. **2D**

Cut the sewn strip units in half vertically. **2E**

Open to reveal (2) 4-patch units. Press. **Make 20. 2F**

Set the 4-patches aside for the moment.

3 make star legs

Place a 5" print square on an angle (any angle) atop a 4½" background square with right sides facing. Make sure your print square is placed a little past the halfway point. Sew ¼" in from the angled edge of the print square. **3A**

Press the piece flat to set the seam, then press the print piece over the seam allowance. **3B**

Turn the unit over and use the background square as a guide to trim the print fabric so that all of the edges are even. Save the trimmed scrap to use for the next star leg. (You should be able to make at least 2 star legs from each print square.) **3C**

Place the trimmed print scrap on the adjacent side of the square. Make sure the edge of the print piece crosses over the first star leg by at least ¼". Stitch ¼" in from the edge of the print piece. **3D**

Press the print piece over the seam allowance. Turn the unit over and use the background square as a guide to trim the print fabric so all of the edges are even. Notice your square is still 4½". **3E**

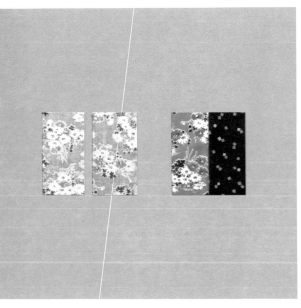

1 Sew down 2 opposite sides of 2 layered 5″ print squares. Cut the sewn squares in half vertically and open to reveal 2 strip units. Press toward the darker fabric.

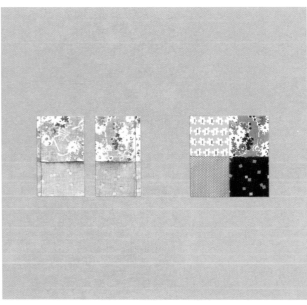

2 With seams running horizontally and right sides together, layer 1 strip unit on top of a differing strip unit. Sew down 2 opposite sides. Cut the sewn strip units in half vertically. Open to reveal (2) 4-patch units. Press. Make 20.

3 Sew a 5″ print square on an angle atop a 4½″ background square with right sides facing. Press the print piece over the seam allowance. Use the background square as a guide to trim the print fabric so that all of the edges are even.

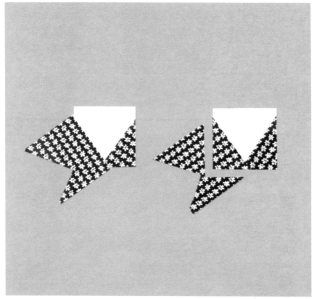

4 Repeat, using the trimmed print scrap to add another star leg to the adjacent edge. Make 80 star leg squares.

5 Sew the squares in 3 rows as shown. Match the seams and sew the rows together to complete the block. Make 20.

Fold the star leg back so the right side of the fabric is facing up and press. **Make 80** star leg squares. **Note:** Have fun with this and don't try to make all of the star legs alike! **3F**

Note: Turn the unit back over so that the right side of the fabric is facing up. Fold the print fabric of the star leg back to reveal the seam allowance and trim the excess background fabric ¼" away from the sewn seam. Fold the star leg back so the right side of the fabric is facing up and press.

4 block construction

Sew a background square to either side of a star leg square. Press the seams towards the background squares.
Make 2. 4A

Sew a star leg square to either side of a 4-patch you set aside earlier, making sure the star legs point away from the 4-patch. Press the seams toward the 4-patch. **4B**

Lay out the star units in 3 rows as shown. **4C**

Nest the seams and sew the rows together to complete the block.
Make 20. 4D

Block Size: 12½" unfinished, 12" finished

5 make horizontal sashing strips

From the background fabric, cut (17) 2½" strips across the width of the fabric. Subcut (3) 2½" x 12½" sashing rectangles from each strip. A **total of (49)** 2½" x 12½" sashing rectangles are needed.

Sew a 2½" print square to the end of (4) 2½" x 12½" rectangles. Sew another 2½" print square to the opposite end of 1 of the units. Sew all the units together to form a row, making sure to alternate between squares and rectangles. Press all of the seams toward the rectangles. **Make 6. 5A**

6 arrange & sew

Lay out the blocks in **5 rows** with each row being made up of **4 blocks**. As you make each row, sew a 2½" x 12½" sashing rectangle between each block and to the beginning and end of the row. Press the seam allowances toward the sashing rectangles. Sew the rows together adding a horizontal sashing strip between each row. Sew a horizontal sashing strip to the top and bottom of the quilt center. Refer to the diagram to your left, if necessary.

7 quilt & bind

Layer the quilt with batting and backing and quilt. After the quilting is complete, square up the quilt and trim away all excess batting and backing. Add binding to complete the quilt. See Construction Basics (pg. 102) for binding instructions.

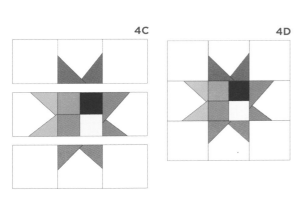

29

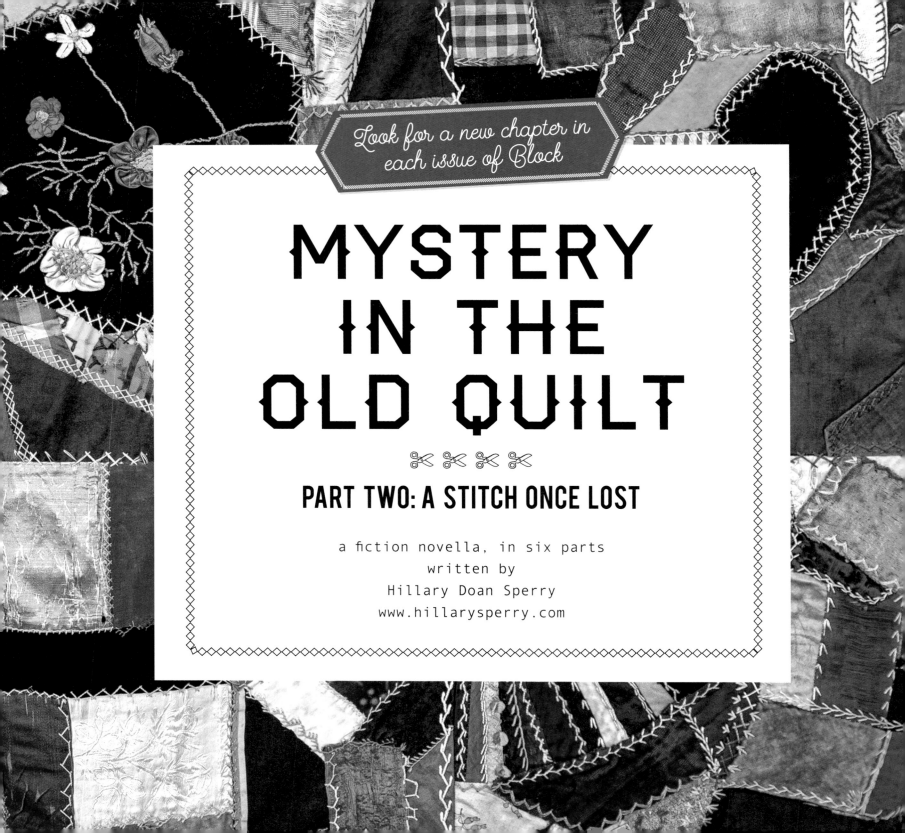

Look for a new chapter in each issue of Block

MYSTERY IN THE OLD QUILT

✄ ✄ ✄ ✄

PART TWO: A STITCH ONCE LOST

a fiction novella, in six parts
written by
Hillary Doan Sperry
www.hillarysperry.com

"Hello, Beautiful." Ron gave Jenny a kiss and slid onto the bench in the outdoor patio opposite Bernie and Dotty. Jenny loved it when he met her at random like this. It didn't hurt that she needed his help. She squeezed his hand and then dug into her purse.

Dotty waved half of her grilled sandwich at Ron. "Have you tried the macadamia-crusted Monte Cristos? They're divine."

"No, but I already had lunch." Ron crumpled a white bag and tossed it onto the table.

Jenny tapped the familiar wrapper with the doorknob she'd pulled from her purse. "I'm not sure you can call Amish fried pies lunch."

"Why not? It had both fruit and grains." Ron took a chip from Jenny's plate. "And now I have veggies."

Jenny pulled her plate away and dropped the doorknob, letting it spin on the metal mesh table top. "This fell off the basement door this morning. Scared me to death! Will you fix it?"

Ron winked and snagged another chip from Jenny's lunch plate. "Of course I will, but you have to be nice."

Bernie snorted. "Jenny has a hard time telling the difference between nice and sassy."

"You're confused." Dotty collected her used paper goods, standing as Claudia Peters approached. "You're the one who gets stuck between sassy and even sassier."

"Hi, Claudia! How are you?" Jenny greeted.

"I'm fine." Claudia dropped to sit on the bench next to Bernie. "My husband has turned my kitchen into a

wasteland, but otherwise, I'm fine."

"A wasteland?" Ron asked.

Claudia nodded, pointing to where the "In a Nut Shell" food truck was parked near the theater. "That's his food truck. He's got it in his head that he wants to cater. So, our kitchen is no longer a kitchen, and he has no idea what he's doing. He keeps hurting himself. He'll be lucky to come out of this remodel with both hands attached."

"Does he need help?" Ron looked across the street to the food truck.

"Well, yes." Claudia gave a strained laugh. "I'm afraid he's bit off more than he can chew."

"I can come by today," Ron said.

"Could you come tomorrow instead? He's not open on Tuesdays."

Ron picked up the stray doorknob Jenny had brought him and nodded. "I'll be there."

"Thank you." Claudia gratefully backed away from the little group. "You should all get some dessert. On the house, er, truck." When no one moved, she gestured for them to follow her. "Here, I'll get it for you. You won't want to miss the peaches and hazelnut cream."

"That's so nice." Jenny stood taking Ron's arm.

Bernie helped Dotty up from the bench. "We have an errand to run, but we'll be back this afternoon for the trunk show. Tell your husband lunch was wonderful."

The two women waved goodbye, and Jenny and Ron followed Claudia across the street.

"He'll be over here," Claudia said, leading them to the back corner of the truck.

Two men argued just out of sight of the customers. Jenny recognized Harold Billet, the owner of the local grocery store, and a larger man who she assumed was Claudia's husband, Sam.

"You're gonna have to be patient," the larger man said in an aggressive whisper. Tension crackled from him. "This is rolling. I'll get your money to you in a couple days."

Harold put his hands up. "I'm not trying to push, Sam, but I've already given you extra time on your order payment. Chanterelles aren't easy to come by so early in the year."

Sam pulled the back door of the trailer open and stepped into the doorway, handing a large manila envelope to the young man in the back and returning to the argument like nothing had happened. "I know. I've only been finding fakes and Jack O'Lantern mushrooms."

"You're kidding, right?" Harold laughed and looked nervously at the group of newcomers. "Those mushrooms are poisonous. You're not cooking with those things, are you? Jacks shouldn't be anywhere near a chef's kitchen. Under the wrong circumstances they'll kill you."

"Of course I'm not. I just wish I could find the real thing. Buying them from you is highway robbery." When all he got was an apologetic shrug, Sam stepped back out and slammed the door. "Fine. Give me an hour. I've still got to clean up here. I'll get the money to you."

"Sam!" Claudia put a hand on her husband's arm. "I was hoping you could fix up some hazelnut creams?

I promised Jenny and Ron."

Sam's face glowed red, but at his wife's touch, he began to relax. By the time he turned to them, he'd almost calmed down completely.

"Of course." Sam patted her hand. "Danny and I can get that ready in a few minutes."

Harold handed Sam a piece of paper. "I'll be at the store until four-thirty."

Sam's smile tightened, and he gave a stiff wave. "I'll see you before then." He took a breath and gave Jenny a wink. "Now, how about some dessert?"

<< >>

Bernie and Dotty walked with Jenny across the deserted street after the late night trunk show. The sun set over the main street, lighting everything from the rose bushes to the visitors in a golden hue. The three women laughed and chatted, grateful for the relief from the oppressive heat of the day.

As they approached the studio, Jenny put a hand out, stopping them in their tracks.

"Did you leave the door open?" she whispered. Dotty shook her head. The basement door creaked in a nonexistent breeze, hanging open on its hinges.

"Me neither." Bernie moved to the side of the building and motioned the other two women closer. Jenny reached for the door just as it flew back. Dotty screamed, and Bernie laughed.

"Jenny?" Ron appeared behind the swinging door.

"What are you doing back there?" Jenny asked, her tone reprimanding.

"Just fixing the doorknob. That's what you wanted me to do when you gave it to me, right?" His eyebrows knitted together as he watched their reactions.

"Yes, of course," Jenny said, feeling guilty for the sharpness of her words. "I was going to show the girls the quilt progress. Do you mind if we go up?" Something moved across the street in the alley by the food truck and Jenny hesitated. "You'll be safe, right?"

"Of course. Will you hand me the screwdriver over there? This one's not long enough." He pinched both sides of the doorknob together, and Jenny retrieved the tool, trading the old one for the one he needed.

She dropped the screwdriver in her purse and motioned for the girls to follow her. "Quick, or he'll have us fetching screws and levels."

Ron scoffed. "It's just a doorknob." He swung the door back and forth a moment, checking some unknown thing. "On second thought. . ."

"Oh my." Dotty hurried past Jenny and up the stairs to the studio.

Jenny followed her with Bernie trailing behind and said, "I thought Bernie was the one who wanted to help."

Jenny opened the door and directed them to the worktable. Dotty shook her head. "She's not helping. Bernie's just excited to know Gina's secret."

Bernie ignored them examining the embroidered squares. When Blair had brought her mother's quilt to Jenny, they'd been tacked in place, but most of it needed to be resewn.

"Think you'll have this fixed by tomorrow?" Jenny teased.

"Can I have 'till the afternoon? It's in quite a state." Bernie pulled a pair of glasses from her handbag and leaned over the blocks. "It's beautiful work, though."

"Embroidery was Gina's specialty," Jenny agreed. Dotty fingered a few of the pins, probably wanting to rearrange things.

"Did you see the poem?" Jenny pointed out the block in question. 'Love again has come to me, love again I must set free.' Got any insights on that?"

Dotty pursed her lips. "Love came and love went. It's possible someone died, or maybe she was married before."

Bernie spoke up. "No. Gina was only married once. I was there."

Jenny raised an eyebrow, and Dotty put a hand on Bernie's shoulder. "Bernie was good friends with Gina's mother, Rachel Moore."

Bernie glared at Dotty as if the knowledge had been privileged information.

"So you would have known her around seventy-four?" Jenny asked, pointing out the dates above and below the poem.

"Well, she definitely didn't get married at that time," Bernie said. "She was still in high school."

"But something happened. Didn't it?" Jenny watched as Bernie shifted her gaze nervously. She was hiding something.

Bernie nodded. "Rachel only talked to me about it a couple times. I was sworn to secrecy."

Dotty narrowed her eyes. "But you've told me, right?"

continued on page 86

For the tutorial and everything you need to make this quilt visit:
www.msqc.co/BlockV7issue2

Crazy Beautiful
Stars & Stitches Quilt

Some days a crazy quilt just makes sense! These old-fashioned beauties are so fascinating with their unique piecing technique; no two are alike. Crazy quilts feature scraps of fabric in a variety of colors and textures, pieced in a manner that resembles a spider web, stained glass, or a cracked piece of pottery. If you look closely, you'll find bits of material that were most likely used to make clothing like calico, velvet, silk, brocade, corduroy, paisley, chenille, satin, and more. It's a snapshot of history.

Suddenly, in the late 1800s, there was access to many different types of fabrics due to advances in transportation, new trade agreements, and the booming textile industry. Crazy quilts showcase that newly available variety with style. With crazy quilts, you get a sense of what people wore and how they repurposed these fabrics and made do with what they had.

Quilters took their scraps and turned this potpourri of fabrics into gorgeous quilts, stitched together with intricate embroidery to show off their needlework skills—often adding unique embellishments like lace, ribbon, buttons, charms, and beads. The decorative stitches were added on each seam using silk thread in a spectrum of colors. These beautiful embroidery stitches took great imagination and ability. They added another dimension of skill to crazy quilts that are admirable all on their own. Crazy quilts are so labor-intensive, it has been estimated that a full-size crazy quilt might have taken over 1,500 hours to finish. That's more than 62 full days of quilting!

Crazy quilts gained widespread popularity in the United States in the late 1800s and the fad lasted until about 1910.

These irregular patchwork quilts were a major departure from traditional geometric quilt designs and were inspired, at least in part, by Japanese artwork found at the Philadelphia Centennial Exposition in 1876. Japanese wares had begun to be imported in 1854 and they were highlighted during the Exposition. At one exhibit, a piece of Japanese artwork created in the traditional "Yosegire" style was showcased. It was a screen created from over 600 pieces of silk and brocade fabric that was unlike anything American quilters had ever seen. This, along with other exhibits showcasing Japanese ceramics and textiles, sparked a national craze.

Nowadays, it's rare to see a crazy quilt in the wild. You might spot one at an antique shop, but they are few and far between due to the delicate nature of Victorian silk and the difficulty of preserving deteriorating fabrics. However, that doesn't mean you can't make your own version of a crazy quilt. It's an excellent way to use up your scraps and an opportunity to really let loose and explore your creativity. Plus, it's a lot easier now that you don't have to hand piece! Give it and go and you may find yourself completely spellbound. There are no rules, no patterns, and no limit to what you can create when you're crazy quilting!

This Stars and Stitches quilt is an interpretation of the asymmetrical piecing you see in crazy quilts but created in a manner that allows you to use a ruler set by Creative Grids called Crazier Eights. These handy, dandy templates are so easy to use. The five simple pieces fit together to create a neatly finished block. It takes out the guesswork for those who don't want to fiddle with odd bits of fabric. Give it a try with your scraps or with a layer cake and have fun with it.

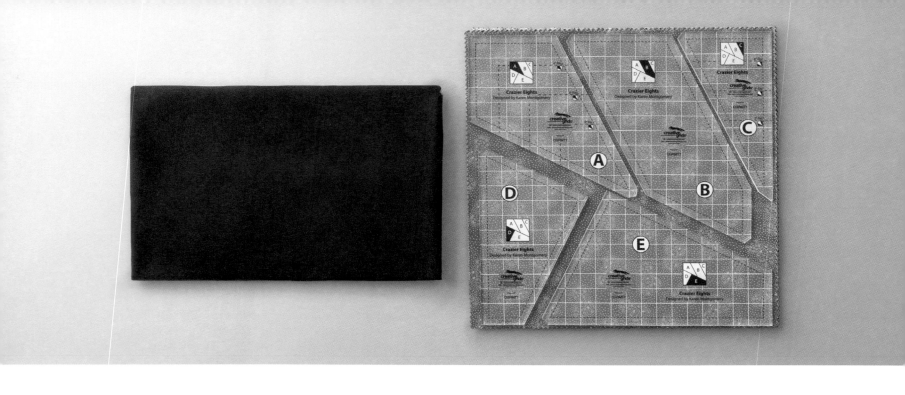

materials

QUILT SIZE
55" x 55"

BLOCK SIZE
16½" unfinished, 16" finished

QUILT TOP
1 package 10" print squares

SASHING & BORDER
1 yard

BINDING
½ yard

BACKING
3½ yards

OTHER
Creative Grids® Crazier Eight
Template Set

SAMPLE QUILT
Esther's Heirloom Shirtings by Kim Diehl
for Henry Glass

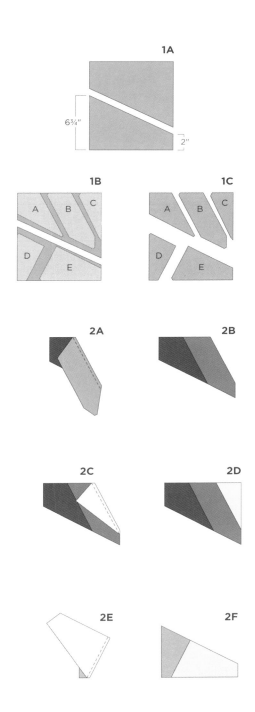

1A

1B   1C

2A   2B

2C   2D

2E   2F

1 cut

Select (6) 10" squares and set them aside for another project.

Place 1 square right side up on your cutting surface.* Measure up from the bottom left corner and mark 6¾" along the left edge. Measure up from the bottom right corner and mark 2" along the right edge. Mark a line between the 2 points and cut the square in 2 sections along the line. **1A**

***Note:** You may wish to stack several 10" squares together, right sides up, and cut them all at 1 time.

Cut pieces A, B, and C from the top section of your fabric square using templates A, B, and C. Cut pieces D and E from the bottom section of your fabric square using templates D and E. **1B**

Repeat the previous instructions to cut pieces A, B, C, D, and E from the remaining squares for a **total of 36** of each. Keep the pieces stacked separately. **Tip:** You may find it helpful to label each stack. **1C**

2 sew quadrants

Select 1 of each piece, making sure the pieces have no matching colors. Lay piece B atop piece A right sides together, as shown. Sew along the matched edges. **2A**

Press the seam allowance toward piece A. **2B**

Lay piece C atop the sewn unit right sides together, as shown. Sew along the matched edges. **2C**

Press the seam allowance toward piece B to complete the top unit. **2D**

Lay piece E atop piece D right sides together, as shown. Sew along the matched edges. **2E**

Press the seam allowance toward piece E to complete the bottom unit. **2F**

Lay the top unit atop the bottom unit right sides together, as shown. Sew along the matched edges. **2G**

Press open to complete 1 quadrant. Repeat to **make 36** quadrants. **2H**

3 block construction

Arrange 4 quadrants in a 4-patch formation as shown, paying close attention to the orientation of the quadrants. Sew the block together in rows. **3A**

Press the seam of the top row to the left and the seam of the bottom row to the right. Nest the seams and sew the rows together. Press to complete the block. **Make 9**. **3B**

Block Size: 16½" unfinished, 16" finished

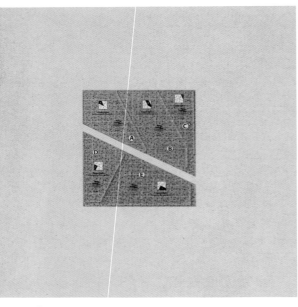

1 Cut pieces A, B, and C from the top section of your fabric square using templates A, B, and C. Cut pieces D and E from the bottom section of your fabric square using templates D and E.

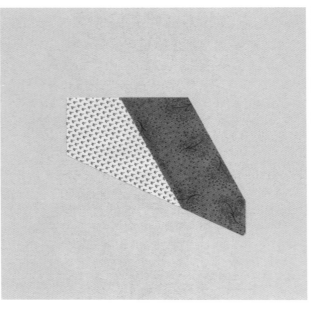

2 Lay piece B atop a different fabric piece A right sides together, lining up right edges. Sew along the matched edges. Press the seam allowance toward piece A.

3 Lay piece C atop the sewn unit right sides together, lining up right edges. Sew along the matched edges. Press the seam allowance toward piece B to complete the top unit.

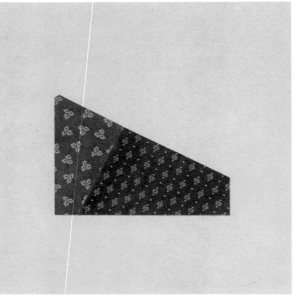

4 Lay piece E atop piece D right sides together, lining up right edges. Sew along the matched edges. Press the seam allowance toward piece E to complete the bottom unit.

5 Lay the top unit atop the bottom unit right sides together, lining up the bottom edges. Sew along the matched edges. Press open to complete 1 quadrant. Make 36 quadrants.

6 Arrange 4 quadrants in a 4-patch formation as shown, paying close attention to the orientation of the quadrants. Sew the block together in rows. Match the seams and sew the rows together. Press to complete the block. Make 9.

4 sashing

From the sashing and border fabric, cut (6) 1½" strips across the width of the fabric. Subcut (2) 1½" x 16½" vertical sashing rectangles from each of 3 strips for a **total of 6** rectangles.

Set the remaining strips aside for the horizontal sashing.

2G

2H

5 arrange & sew

Referring to the diagram on your left, lay out your blocks in **3 rows** of **3 blocks** each. Sew the blocks together with a vertical sashing rectangle between each block to create the rows. **5A**

Sew the 3 strips set aside earlier end-to-end to create 1 long strip.

Measure the width of your rows to determine the length of your horizontal sashing, approximately 50½". Cut the long sashing strip into 2 strips that are the same width as your rows. Sew the rows together with a horizontal sashing strip between each row to complete the quilt center.

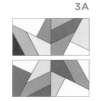
3A

3B

5A

6 border

From the border fabric, cut (6) 3" strips across the width of the fabric. Sew the strips end-to-end to create 1 long strip. Trim the border from this strip.

Refer to Borders (pg. 102) in the Construction Basics to measure and cut the border. The strips are approximately 50½" for the sides and approximately 55½" for the top and bottom.

7 quilt & bind

Layer the quilt with batting and backing and quilt. After the quilting is complete, square up the quilt and trim away all excess batting and backing. Add binding to complete the quilt. See Construction Basics (pg. 102) for binding instructions.

What's All The Fuss All About?

It's okay to be a little fussy when it comes to fabric! If you've never heard the term fussy cutting before, it might sound like it's tough to do, but it couldn't be simpler. Fussy cutting is all about showcasing your favorite prints by cutting the fabric in a way that allows you to emphasize a specific part of the motif. Have you ever found a print you absolutely adore? It might be perfect for fussy cutting because you'll take the care to place it well within a quilt block so you can admire it forever. In this case, precuts aren't always the way to go because they have already been cut without regard to the print, so it's best to work with yardage.

Fussy cutting isn't just about taking a cute motif and placing it front and center. It can also be used strategically to be sure stripes, plaids, and ginghams line up, use prints to their fullest potential, and make colors really shine. It really takes piecing quilt blocks to the next level. You might even be doing it already without knowing it. Fussy cutting is all about being more thoughtful when you cut into fabric. When it's used well, the results can be absolutely stunning!

One place where you'll see a lot of fussy cutting is in English paper piecing. Those darling hexagons are just begging to showcase a special print. And when you put English paper pieced shapes together just so, it can look like a kaleidoscope!

When you have a pattern that lends itself to fussy cutting, you'll want to decide which parts of the print you want to focus on. In this case, we are using the Disappearing Nine-Patch block, and it gives you four opportunities to showcase cute prints. You'll want to piece them into each of the four corners so they won't be cut into when you create the block.

When the preliminary block is cut and rearranged, the finished result is so darling! The fussy cut squares stand out and the prints are showcased in a unique way. There are so many ways to use fussy cutting and it transforms the way you look at prints. What can you do with fussy cutting? Share your projects with us at **#msqcshowandtell.**

Fussy cutting tips:

- Always leave at least ¼″ inch of space around your motif so that none of it ends up in the seam allowance.

- Fussy cutting uses up more fabric, so make sure to buy an extra yard or two. You'll end up with more scraps, but save them for other projects!

- When you fussy cut, the motifs may end up on the bias, so it's a good idea to starch your fabric before you cut it and handle it carefully to avoid distorting your print.

- Use a see-through ruler to be sure you're cutting exactly where you want to and avoid accidentally cutting off an important part of your print.

- A smaller rotary cutter also helps. Consider sizing down to a 28mm for more accurate fussy cutting.

Create a Fuss

Well-placed prints come to life in these Disappearing 9-Patch blocks. The sashing frames the motifs for added emphasis. See pg. 68 for piecing instructions.

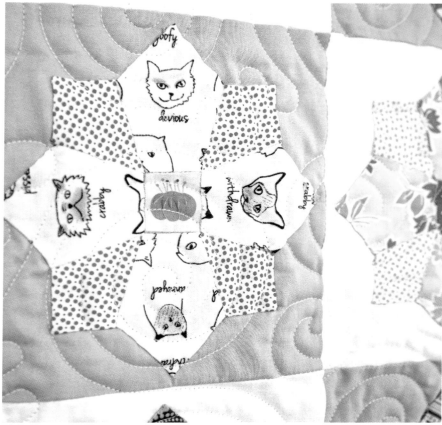

Try a Template

Clear fussy cutting templates in graduated sizes make selecting the perfect motif easy. Be sure to note the marked ¼" inch around the edge. It helps you know what the finished size of the block will be to ensure no part of your image will end up in the seam.

For the tutorial and everything you need to make this quilt visit:

www.msqc.co/BlockV7issue2

Make it Modern, Make it Traditional, Make it Yours
Wonder Quilt featuring Katie Larson

Explore a wonderland of amazing angles in Katie Larson's latest modern quilt. This fresh pattern in a contemporary palette has plenty of aqua, pink, orange, yellow, cerulean, and navy, with gray and white accents for a bit of breathing room. We took a moment to chat with Katie about her clever creation and this is what she had to say.

Can you tell us a little bit about yourself and how you got into quilting?

"I love being creative, from doing graphic design as a career to all different types of crafts. Quilting is one of my favorites, and I have been doing it for 20+ years. My mom was a quilter, and she passed her love of it to me!"

What inspired you to make this quilt? Why is it called "Wonder"?

"This quilt was inspired by my recent fabric collection with Paintbrush Studio Fabrics called 'Wonder.' I was drawn to bright colors and bold shapes, and the excitement of seeing something new for the first time. I created a quilt block that can be rotated and reflected in different ways, which creates a medallion style quilt. The look of a pattern can change so much by the way you place the blocks and the colors you choose."

What colors do you like to quilt with the most? What influences your color choices?

"I love bright colors. They are what I gravitate to most at a quilt shop and in life! Aqua is my favorite, and it usually ends up making its way into my home and most of my quilts."

What techniques do you enjoy using the most when quilting? Do you have any tips or tricks for those who will make your quilt?

"I love working with angles (and I love how they look in quilts), but they can also be tricky! I will often mark the ¼" in each corner of a piece, and use those marks to line up and pin to ensure I'm sewing the pieces correctly."

What else would you like to add about your quilt?

"I initially used several different materials in this quilt—flannel, quilting cotton, woven cotton, satin, and linen—to provide a variety of textures. Try using a mix of fabrics to give the quilt a great feel."

Traditional Palette

Try Wonder in a traditional palette for a quilt that's sure to dazzle. Stitched up in beautiful Desert Sun Batiks with warm yellows and oranges offset by cool teal, blue, and purple, it's filled with island appeal. Just by changing the fabrics from solids to batiks, the tone of the quilt shifts completely. One pattern can have infinite possibilities! This design lends itself well to interpretation because it is made up of simple shapes. Wonder can feel modern in bold, crisp colors, playful in cute prints, or classic in traditional prints. It's all up to you!

materials - Wonder

QUILT SIZE
72" x 72"

BLOCK SIZE
36½" unfinished, 36" finished

QUILT TOP
½ yard - navy fabric
¾ yard - light blue, red, yellow, light gray,
    and dark gray fabrics
1¼ yards - purple, teal, cream, and pink
    fabrics

BINDING
¾ yard

BACKING
4½ yards - vertical seam(s)
    or 2¼ yards of 108" wide

SAMPLE QUILT
Solid fabrics from various manufacturers

materials - variation

QUILT SIZE
72" x 72"

BLOCK SIZE
36½" unfinished, 36" finished

QUILT TOP
½ yard - FBY-81445
¾ yard - FBY-81446, FBY-81444,
    FBY-81455, FBY-81453, Background
1¼ yards - FBY-81457, FBY-81450,
    FBY-81447, FBY-81452

BINDING
¾ yard

BACKING
4½ yards - vertical seam(s)
    or 2¼ yards of 108" wide

SAMPLE QUILT
Desert Sun by Island Batik

fabric key

WONDER VERSION	TRADITIONAL VERSION
Purple	FBY-81457
Navy	FBY-81445
Teal	FBY-81450
Lt. Blue	FBY-81446
Cream	FBY-81447
Pink	FBY-81452
Red	FBY-81444
Yellow	FBY-81455
Lt. Gray	FBY-81453
Dark Gray/ Background	White

1 cut

From the **purple** fabric:
- Cut a 10″ strip across the width of the fabric. Subcut the strip into (2) 10″ squares.

- Cut (2) 9½″ strips across the width of the fabric. Subcut (4) 9½″ squares from 1 strip and (2) 9½″ squares from the second. Subcut (2) 9½″ squares once on the diagonal to yield (4) 9½″ triangles.

- Cut (2) 5″ strips across the width of the fabric. From each strip, subcut (2) 5″ x 14″ rectangles.

From the **navy** fabric:
- Cut a 10″ strip across the width of the fabric. Subcut the strip into (4) 10″ squares.

- Cut a 5″ strip across the width of the fabric. Subcut the strip into (4) 5″ x 9½″ rectangles.

From the **teal** fabric:
- Cut a 19″ strip across the width of the fabric. Subcut (1) 19″ square from the strip. Trim the remainder of the strip to 10″. Subcut (2) 10″ squares.

- Cut a 9½″ strip across the width of the fabric. Subcut (4) 9½″ squares.

- Cut a 5″ strip across the width of the fabric. Set the strip aside to make a strip set.

From the **light blue** fabric:
- Cut a 10″ strip across the width of each fabric. Subcut (2) 10″ squares.

* Cut (2) 5″ strips across the width of the fabric and set 1 strip aside to make a strip set. Subcut the remaining strip into (4) 5″ x 9½″ rectangles.

- Cut a 5″ strip across the width of the fabric. Set the strip aside for making a strip set.

From the **cream** fabric:
* Cut a 10″ strip across the width of the fabric. Subcut (2) 10″ squares and (2) 10″ x 9½″ rectangles. Cut each rectangle in half to yield (4) 5″ x 9½″ rectangles.

- Cut (3) 9½″ strips across the width of the fabric. Subcut (4) 9½″ squares from 1 strip. From each of the 2 remaining strips, subcut (2) 9½″ x 18½″ rectangles.

From the **pink** fabric:
- Cut a 10″ strip across the width of the fabric. Subcut (2) 10″ squares.

- Cut (3) 9½″ strips across the width of the fabric. Subcut (4) 9½″ squares from 1 strip. From each of the remaining 2 strips, subcut (2) 9½″ x 18½″ rectangles.

From the **red** fabric:
* Cut a 9½″ strip across the width of the fabric. Subcut (4) 9½″ squares.

- Cut (2) 5″ strips across the width of the fabric. From each strip, subcut (2) 5″ x 9½″ rectangles and (2) 5″ squares.

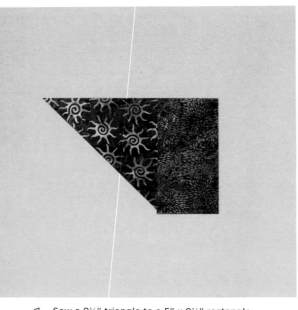

1 Sew a 9½" triangle to a 5" x 9½" rectangle. Press the seam toward the triangle.

2 Sew a 5" triangle to the bottom of the unit. Press the seam toward the triangle. Set this aside for a moment.

3 Follow the instructions on page 47 to create an 18½" half-square triangle and cut it in half on the diagonal.

4 Pick up the pieced triangle unit you set aside above and place it atop a portion of the half-square triangle, as shown. Sew along the slanted edge.

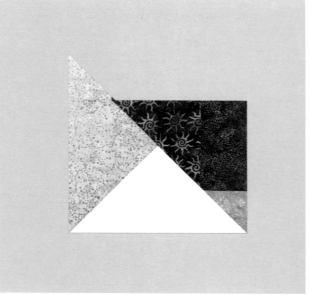

5 Open the unit and press the seam toward the half-square triangle.

6 Use the top of the pieced triangle unit to trim the top of the half-square triangle even with the rest of the block.

48

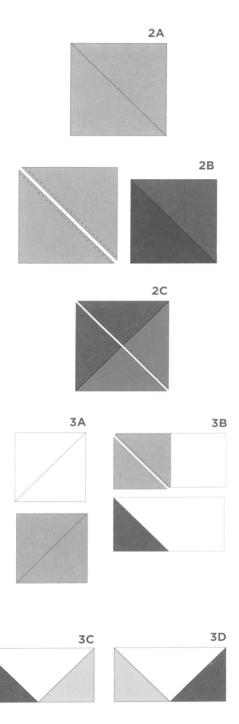

From the **yellow** fabric:

- Cut a 9½" strip across the width of the fabric. Subcut (4) 9½" squares from the strip.

- Cut (2) 5" strips across the width of the fabric. Subcut each strip into (2) 5" x 14" rectangles and (1) 5" square. Cut each square in half once on the diagonal to yield (4) 5" triangles.

From the **light gray** fabric:

- Cut a 10" strip across the width of the fabric. Subcut (2) 10" squares from the strip.

- Cut (2) 5" strips across the width of the fabric. From each strip, subcut (2) 5" x 9½" rectangles and (2) 5" squares.

From the **dark gray** fabric:

- Cut a 19" strip across the width of the fabric. Subcut (1) 19" square from the strip.

2 make half-square triangles

Draw a diagonal line once corner to corner on the reverse side of a 10" teal square. **2A**

Lay the marked square on top of a 10" purple square, right sides facing. Sew on both sides of the marked line using a ¼" seam allowance. Cut on the marked line and open to reveal 2 half-square triangles. Press the seam allowance of each unit toward the darker fabric. Repeat to make a **total of 4** teal/purple half-square triangles. **2B**

Repeat the previous steps using (2) 10" light blue squares and (2) 10" navy

squares to make a **total of 4** light blue/navy half-square triangles.

In a similar manner, pair (2) 10" light gray squares with (2) 10" navy squares and (2) 10" cream squares with (2) 10" pink squares to make a **total of 4** light gray/navy half-square triangles and a **total of 4** cream/pink half-square triangles.

Trim each half-square triangle unit to 9½".

Pair the 19" teal and dark gray squares and repeat the steps to create a **total of 2** teal/dark gray half-square triangles. These half-square triangles are larger than the rest, but the process to create the half-square triangles is the same. These larger half-square triangles should each be trimmed to 18½".

Cut each of the large teal/dark gray half-square triangles once on the diagonal. We'll refer to these as teal/dark gray triangles. **2C**

3 make flying geese

Draw a diagonal line once corner to corner on the reverse side (4) 9½" teal squares and (4) 9½" pink squares. **3A**

Lay a marked teal square on the left side of a cream 9½" x 18½" rectangle with right sides facing, as shown. Sew on the marked line to snowball the corner of the rectangle. Trim the excess fabric ¼" away from the sewn seam. Press the seam allowance toward the snowballed corner. **3B**

Tip: If you'd like, you can sew another seam ½" away from the marked line on the side nearest the corner of the rectangle when snowballing these corners. Then, cut between the stitch lines and you'll end up with a bonus half-square triangle from each snowballed corner that you can use for another project.

Use a marked pink square and repeat the previous instructions to snowball the lower right corner of the unit. **Make 2** cream/teal/pink flying geese units. **3C**

Make 2 mirrored cream/teal/pink flying geese units by simply reversing the placement of the fabrics when snowballing the corners of the rectangle. **3D**

Use previous steps to **make 2** pink/cream/red flying geese units and to **make 2** mirrored pink/cream/red flying geese units.

4 make strip squares

Pick up the light blue and teal strips. Place them 1 on top of the other with right sides facing and sew them together along 1 long edge. Open and press toward the darker fabric. Cut the sewn strip set into (4) 9½" segments that we'll refer to as strip squares. **4A**

5 make pieced rectangles

On the reverse side of (2) 5" x 14" yellow rectangles, draw a 45° line beginning in the bottom right corner of the rectangle as shown. **5A**

Place a marked rectangle on top of a 5" x 9½" light blue rectangle as shown.

Sew on the marked line. Trim the excess fabric ¼" away from the sewn seam. Open and press the seam allowance toward the darker fabric. **Make 2** yellow/light blue pieced rectangles. **5B 5C**

On 2 additional 5" x 14" yellow rectangles, draw a 45° line beginning in the bottom left corner of the rectangle as shown. **5D**

Place a marked rectangle on top of a 5" x 9½" light blue rectangle as shown. Sew on the marked line. Trim the excess fabric ¼" away from the sewn seam. Open and press the seam allowance toward the darker fabric. **Make 2** mirrored yellow/light blue pieced rectangles. **5E 5F**

Use the 5" x 14" purple rectangles and 5" x 9½" light gray rectangles to **make 2** purple/light gray pieced rectangles and **make 2** mirrored purple/light gray pieced rectangles.

6 make snowballed rectangles

Draw a diagonal line once corner to corner on the reverse side of (4) 5" red squares. **6A**

Lay a marked square on the left side of a 5" x 9½" cream rectangle with right sides facing, as shown. Sew on the marked line to snowball the corner of the rectangle. Trim the excess fabric ¼" away from the sewn seam. Press the seam allowance toward the snowballed corner. **Make 2** red/cream rectangles. **6B**

Lay a marked square on the right side of 5" x 9½" cream rectangle with right

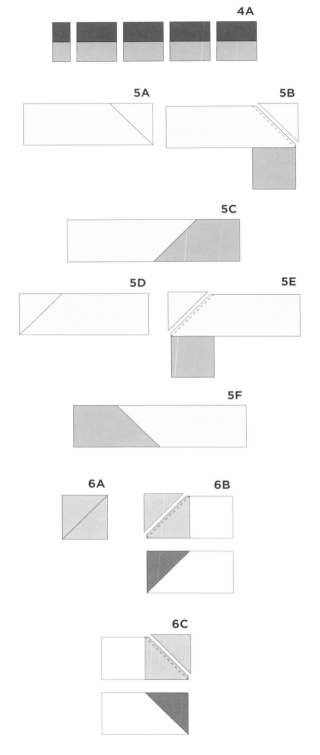

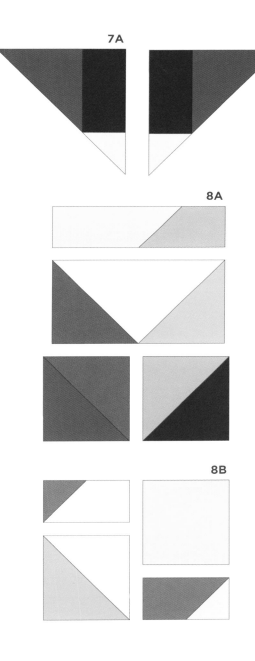

7A **7B**

8A

8B

sides facing, as shown. Sew on the marked line to snowball the corner of the rectangle. Trim the excess fabric and press the seam allowance toward the snowballed corner. **Make 2** mirrored red/cream rectangles. **6C**

Use the 5" x 9½" red rectangles and the 5" light gray squares and follow the steps above to **make 2** light gray/red rectangles and **make 2** mirrored light gray/red rectangles.

7 make pieced triangles

Pick up the 9½" purple triangles, 5" x 9½" navy rectangles, and (4) 5" yellow triangles. Sew a purple triangle to the left side of a rectangle and press the seam towards the triangle. Sew a yellow triangle to the bottom of the unit and press the seam towards the triangle. **Make 2** pieced triangles. **7A**

Sew a purple triangle to the right side of a rectangle and press the seam towards the triangle. Sew a yellow triangle to the bottom of the unit and press the seam towards the triangle. **Make 2** mirrored pieced triangles. **7B**

8 block construction

Sew a teal/purple half-square triangle to the left side of a light blue/navy half-square triangle. Press the seam toward the darker fabric. Sew a cream/teal/pink flying geese unit to the top of the half-square triangles and press the seam toward the bottom. Sew a yellow/light blue pieced rectangle to the top of the unit and press the seams toward

the bottom. We'll call this Section 1 for clarity. **Make 2**. **8A**

Sew a red/cream rectangle to the top of a cream/pink half-square triangle. Sew a 9½" yellow square to the top of a light gray/red rectangle. Press the seam of both units toward the bottom. Sew the first unit to the left of the second unit. Press the seam to the left. We'll call this Section 2 for clarity. **Make 2**. **8B**

Sew a teal/dark gray triangle to a pieced triangle unit as shown. Press the seam toward the teal/dark gray triangle. **8C**

Use the top of the pieced triangle as a guide to trim the teal/dark gray triangle. This completes this section of the block and we'll call it Section 3 for clarity. **Make 2**. **8D**

Sew a light gray/navy half-square triangle to the top of a strip square. Press the seam toward the strip square. Sew a pink/cream/red flying geese unit to the left side of the unit. Press the seam toward the right. Sew a purple/light gray pieced mirrored rectangle* to the bottom of the unit. Press toward the bottom. We'll call this Section 4 for clarity. **Make 2**. **8E**

***Note:** This block uses the mirrored pieced rectangle you created. The mirrored blocks you'll make later will use the purple/light gray pieced rectangles. Be sure to consult the diagram when assembling this section to ensure you are using the correct pieces.*

Sew Section 1 to the top of Section 2 and press the seam toward the bottom. Sew Section 3 to the top of Section 4 and press the seam toward the top. Sew the Section 1/Section 2 unit to the left of the Section 3/Section 4 unit and press the seam ward the right. **Make 2. 8F 8G**

Use the mirrored units you created to **make 2** mirrored blocks in a similar manner. **8H**

Block Size: 36½" unfinished, 36" finished

9 arrange & sew

Arrange the blocks in **2 rows** of **2 blocks** as shown in the diagram on page 51. Sew the blocks together in pairs to form rows. Press the seam of the top row to the right and the seam of the bottom row to the left. Nest the seams and sew the rows together to complete the quilt top.

10 quilt & bind

Layer the quilt with batting and backing and quilt. After the quilting is complete, square up the quilt and trim away all excess batting and backing. Add binding to complete the quilt. See Construction Basics (pg. 102) for binding instructions.

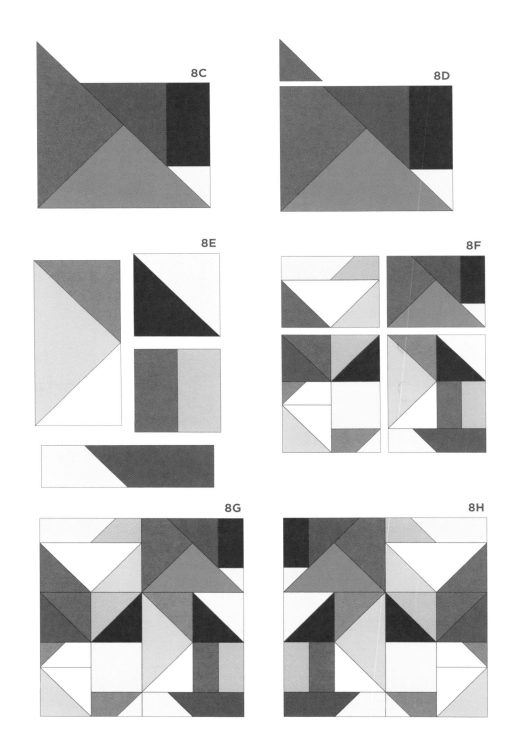

*For the tutorial and everything
you need to make this quilt visit:*
www.msqc.co/BlockV7issue2

Take the Scenic Route
Road Trip Quilt

How far have you gone for your quilts? For some quilters, a trip into town to the fabric shop is all they need, or maybe you've made the trip out to Hamilton to visit us, but others take it even further!

Lately, there's been a popular fad of quilters taking their quilts out into nature and photographing them in places you wouldn't normally expect to see quilts. By surrounding their geometric patterns with nature, these quilters are taking juxtaposition to the next level!

There are thousands of examples of "Quilts in the Wild" all across the internet, ranging from beachside sawtooth star quilts to brightly colored chevron quilts in the midsts of snowy forests! As the colors and the environment collide, our artistic minds just light up with delight as we take in the beautiful contrast.

Sometimes, these posts are as simple as taking their quilt out onto the back porch and posing it, but some quilters are taking long road trips just to get the perfect pic of their quilt in the wild. Why settle for a scene you see out the back window every day when you can make a trip of it, taking photos and making memories you'll treasure for a long time?

One woman made a quilt featuring the landscapes of Yosemite National Park and then drove all the way there to pose her quilt with the real deal. Another took her quilt overseas and posed in the Black Forest of Germany. Now that's dedication to the art.

Of course, sometimes the journey is more important than the destination. When my kids were growing up, we used to drive from our home in Missouri all the way back to California to visit my parents. Now, that's a hefty drive, and you've got to keep your mind occupied, right? I would prep a few little sewing projects before we'd leave, and then I'd sew from the passenger seat of our car all the way there! While it wasn't as efficient as my sewing machine (it's a bit hard to bring a sewing machine along in the car), it sure helped to keep my mind off of the rowdy kids in the back seat!

Having seen all these fantastic posts online, we'd love to ask: How far has quilting taken you? Share your travel quilting stories with us on Facebook or Instagram with the tag **#msqcshowandtell**. We're always excited to hear stories from all our fans. And, if you haven't done something like this yet, maybe this will be your inspiration to go on a quilting road trip! So, go out there and make some quilts, and some memories that you'll treasure for years to come.

materials

QUILT SIZE
72" x 81½"

BLOCK SIZE
10" unfinished, 9½" finished

QUILT TOP
1 package 10" print squares
1 package 10" background squares

INNER BORDER
¾ yard

OUTER BORDER
1½ yards

BINDING
¾ yard

BACKING
5 yards - vertical seam(s) or 2½ yards 108" wide

OTHER
2¾ yards Heat n Bond Lite

SAMPLE QUILT
Fiddle Dee Dee by Me & My Sister Designs for Moda Fabrics

4A

4B

4C

1 cut

Cut the fusible web into 8½" strips across the width. Subcut the strips into 8½" squares. Each strip will yield 2 squares and a **total of 21** are needed.

2 trace

Use the templates found at **msqc.co/ roadtriptemplate.**

Select the 21 states you wish to include in your quilt. Trace the outlines of the selected states onto the paper side of the fusible web squares. Each of the outlines have been reversed for your convenience. **Make 21.**

3 fuse & cut

Select a 10" print square. Place the fusible web on the wrong side of the fabric with the glue side touching. Following the manufacturer's instructions, iron the fusible web to the fabric. Cut out the state on the traced line. **Make 21**.

4 make the blocks

Pick up 1 cut state and a 10" background square. Carefully peel the paper backing off. Place the state in the center of a 10" background square. Again, follow the manufacturer's instructions for the fusible web to adhere the state to the background square. **4A**

Stitch around the edge of the state using a small blanket or zigzag stitch. **4B** **Make 21** blocks.

Block Size: 9½" finished

Bonus: Is there a location on your quilt you'd like to show a little extra love? We've included a heart outline on the last page of our templates. Trace the heart onto a scrap of fusible web and follow the same steps to adhere and sew it to your block. **4C**

5 arrange & sew

Refer to the diagram on page 57 and lay out the blocks and remaining 10" print squares in rows. Each row is made up of **6 blocks** and **7 rows** are needed. Sew the blocks into rows. After they have been sewn into rows, press the seam allowance of the odd-numbered rows to the right and the even-numbered rows to the left to make the seams nest.

Sew the rows together to complete the center of the quilt.

6 inner border

Cut (7) 2½" strips from the inner border fabric. Sew the strips together end-to-end to make 1 long strip. Trim the borders from this strip.

Refer to Borders (pg. 102) in the Construction Basics to measure and cut the inner borders. The strips

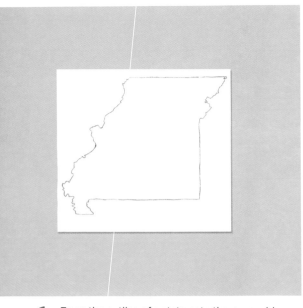

1 Trace the outline of a state onto the paper side of a square of fusible web.

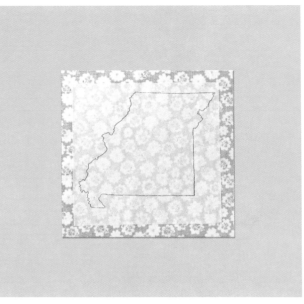

2 Adhere the fusible web square with the traced outline onto the wrong side of a 10" print square.

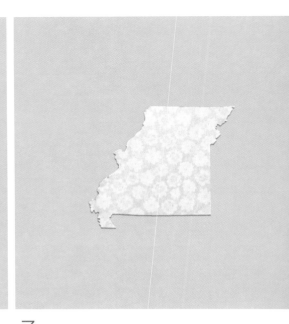

3 Cut out the appliqué shape on the traced line.

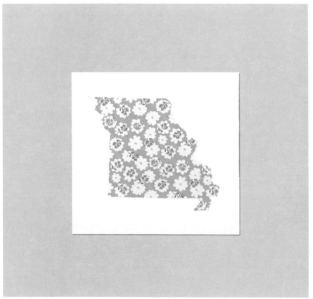

4 Peel off the paper backing of the fusible web. Center the appliqué shape onto a 10" square of background fabric. Adhere the appliqué shape to the background square.

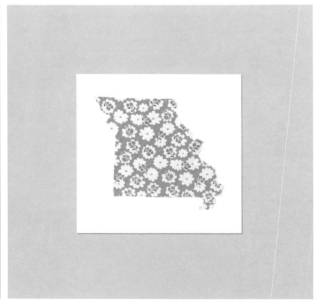

5 Stitch around the raw edge of the appliqué shape using a small blanket or zigzag stitch to complete the block.

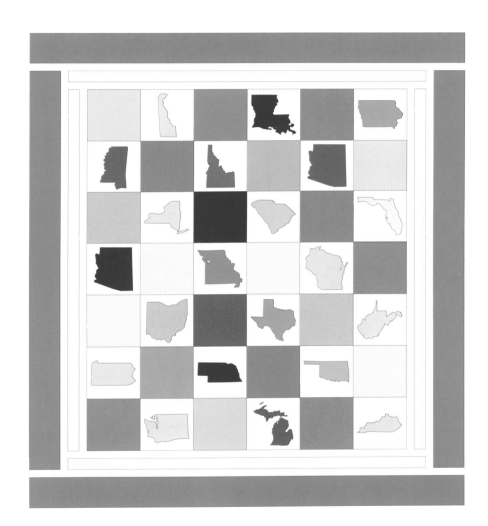

are approximately 67" for the sides and approximately 61½" for the top and bottom.

7 outer border

Cut (8) 6" strips from the outer border fabric. Sew the strips together end-to-end to make 1 long strip. Trim the borders from this strip.

Refer to Borders (pg. 102) in the Construction Basics to measure and cut the inner borders. The strips are approximately 71" for the sides and approximately 72½" for the top and bottom.

8 quilt & bind

Layer the quilt with batting and backing and quilt. After the quilting is complete, square up the quilt and trim away all excess batting and backing. Add binding to complete the quilt. See Construction Basics (pg. 102) for binding instructions.

1 cut

From the border fabric, cut:
- Cut (2) 2½" strips across the width of the fabric. Subcut (1) 2½" x 16" rectangle and (1) 2½" x 12" rectangle from each strip.
- Cut an 11" strip across the width of the fabric. Subcut (2) 11" x 16" rectangles and set the rest of the fabric aside for another project.

From the background fabric, cut:
- Cut a 12" wide strip along the length of the fabric. Subcut a 12" square from the strip of fabric.
- Cut an 18" square from the remainder of the fabric to use as the backing square for your pillow top.

materials

PROJECT SIZE
Fits a 16" pillow form

BLOCK SIZE
12" unfinished, 11½" finished

PROJECT SUPPLIES
(16) 2½" print squares
½ yard coordinating fabric
  - includes borders and pillow back
½ yard background fabric

OTHER
8½" square of Heat n Bond Lite
17" square of batting

OPTIONAL PILLOW INSERT
½ yard muslin
Fiberfill

2 sew

Select (4) 2½" squares and arrange them in a 4-patch formation. Sew the squares together in pairs to form rows. Press the seam of the top row to the right and the bottom row to the left. **Make (4)** 4-patch units. **2A**

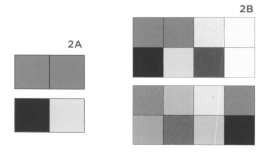

2A

2B

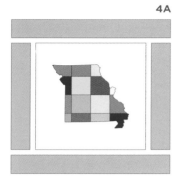

4A

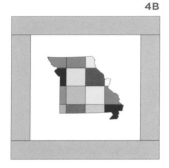

4B

5A

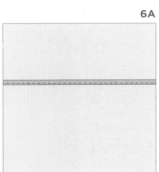

6A

Arrange your 4-patch units into 2 rows of 2 units to create a larger 4-patch. Sew the units together in pairs to form rows. Press the seam of the top row to the right and the bottom row to the left. **2B**

Note: All of the templates will fit on the patchwork we have outlined above, but you may be able to use fewer 2½" squares to create your patchwork depending on the state you choose. If you'd like, you can measure the outline of your chosen state and make adjustments to the number of squares you sew together. **2B**

3 appliqué
Note: The appliqué portion of this pillow project uses the same method as the Road Trip Quilt project. Instead of using a 10" print square to create the appliqué shape, use the patchwork you made above. Use the 12" background square in place of the 10" background square used to create the blocks within the quilt.

Print the templates for your project from **http://msqc.co/roadtriptemplate** Follow the steps to trace, fuse, cut, and make the block as found on page 55.

Block Size: 12" unfinished, 11½" finished

4 pillow top
Sew a 2½" x 12" rectangle to either side of your completed appliqué block. Press the seams toward the rectangles. Sew a 2½" x 16" rectangle to the top and bottom of the unit. Press the seams toward the rectangles to complete the pillow front. **4A 4B**

Layer your pillow top on top of the batting and backing square. Baste and quilt using your favorite methods. After the quilting is complete, square up and trim away all excess batting and backing.

5 pillow back
Fold a long edge of an 11" x 16" rectangle over ½" with wrong sides touching. Press. Repeat a second time to enclose the raw edge of the fabric. Topstitch along the folded edge. Repeat on 1 edge of the remaining rectangle to create the 2 pillow back flaps. **5A**

6 finish the pillow
Lay the pillow top with the right side facing up. Lay the 2 pillow back flaps on top of the pillow top. **6A**

Note: The right sides of the pillow back flaps should be touching the right side of the pillow top and the pillow back flaps should overlap each other by about 4".

Pin or clip the pillow back flaps to the pillow top. Sew around the perimeter of the pillow using a ¼" seam allowance. Finish the edges with a serger or zigzag stitch to prevent fraying.

Clip the corners and turn the pillow right sides out. Insert a pillow form to finish your project or stuff the pillow with fiberfill and whipstitch the opening closed.

Spring Clean
Your Machine

"The objective of cleaning is not just to clean, but to feel happiness living within that environment."

-Marie Kondo

Spring cleaning. The words either make you excited to start fresh or fill you with a feeling of dread. And, honestly, it all depends on my mood. There eventually will be a special Saturday that comes along in early spring. I'll finally see buds on my tree and hear birds singing and suddenly I'll be hit with the urge to dig in and tackle my messy sewing room. Like I said, it doesn't happen often, but when it does, you'd better watch out because I'll clean every nook and cranny and if anyone gets in the way, they'll get dusted off, too!

Step 1 - Remove your needle and replace it with a new, sharp one when you're all through cleaning your machine.

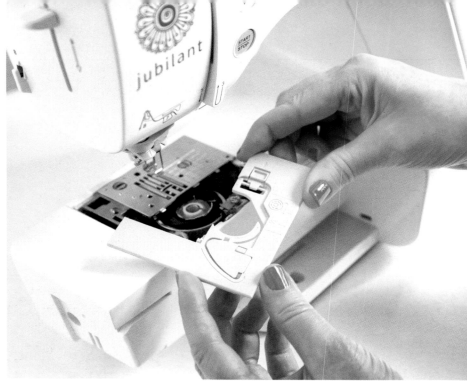

Step 2 - Remove the top plates on you machine.

Now, let's get real. Have you ever cleaned your sewing machine? Not just dusting off the outside. Have you cracked it open and cleaned inside? Gulp. I finally got the guts to do it and I was shocked. My bobbin looked like a bird's nest! But don't worry. It's totally doable and I'll walk you through it.

Before you start, unplug your machine and remove the needle. More often than not, your needle needs to be replaced anyhow—the rule of thumb is after about every 8 hours of sewing—so let's go ahead and take it out and chuck it. Next up, we're going to dust the machine before we oil it. Do you remember that funky little nylon brush that came with your sewing machine? Now's the time to dig it out and finally use it! It's not recommended to use a can of spray air because it can lodge dust and moisture deeper into crevices and cause problems later on. Thoroughly brush off all the dust on the outside of your machine first. Then, we'll go deeper!

Keep the dust bunnies at bay and cover your machine when it's not in use. If you don't have a cover, sew one in your favorite fabric! And be sure to use high-quality thread when sewing. It produces less lint and runs smoothly through your machine.

If you've got a pipe cleaner lying around, you can use it to clean your tension disks. Unthread your machine, make sure the foot is up, and then take your pipe cleaner and gently run it through the thread guide and around the tension control knob, if your machine has one. There can be some lint buildup there. Next up, brush off your presser foot and the surrounding area.

Then, remove your presser foot and the needle plate with that special short screwdriver or a dime. Inside you'll find the motherlode! If you've never opened up this part of your machine, there will be plenty of fuzz and thread. Dust off the feed dogs and then you should be able to pop out your bobbin case and actually clean underneath it. Don't forget to clean off the actual bobbin case as well.

Now it's time to oil your machine. Some manufacturers tell you not to oil your machine and to take it in for maintenance. If that's the case, you're all done! If your machine could use a little TLC, go ahead and add a small drop of oil to the shelf that your bobbin case sits on before you replace it so it moves smoothly. Check your machine manual to see if there are any additional spots that can be oiled and that's it! And be careful not to add additional oil where it shouldn't be. Once your machine is clean and dusted with a fresh needle in place, you're ready to start on a brand new sewing project just in time for spring!

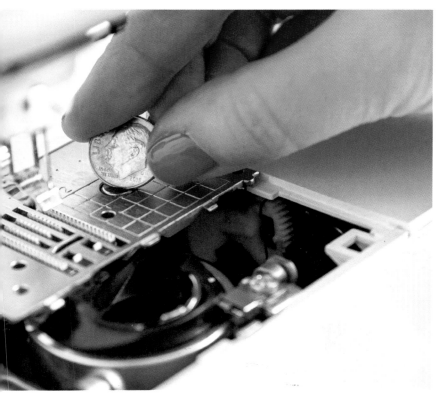

Step 3 - Try using a dime to unscrew those tricky sections. It fits perfectly and small enough to get into those tight spots.

Step 4 - Use a brush or lint catcher to help get all the dust bunnies out of your machine.

For the tutorial and everything
you need to make this quilt visit:
www.msqc.co/BlockV7issue2

Rainbow Quilts *by Mary Green*

Disappearing Nine-Patch Windowpane Quilt

Rainbows signify hope and I smile every single time I see one. When the clouds finally break after a rainstorm, I'm always on the lookout for a beautiful rainbow arching across the gray sky. In life, we all experience cloudy moments and it can be hard to stay positive. This story of quilting through a time of loss by one of our readers, Mary Green, touched my heart and reminded me to always look for rainbows in life.

"I had only been quilting, if you want to call it that, for less than a year when I found out I was pregnant at the end of 2016. I was all geared up to make a baby quilt for my new arrival and turned to Missouri Star on YouTube to teach me how to make one properly. Sadly though, I lost my baby girl 18 weeks into my pregnancy. The little blanket I had started for her, I finished quickly and had with me to wrap her in at delivery. I cherish that I was able to give her at least one present from Mom.

"In the months that followed, I found out I was pregnant again. I decided this time to make a rainbow-colored quilt for my soon-to-be rainbow baby. I watched many Missouri Star tutorials before getting started because I wanted to get it right! Plenty of time and money was spent getting beautiful fabrics in every color of the rainbow. After I had made it through the first trimester of this pregnancy, it was time to get started on the rainbow quilt. I only made it through the beginning stages of my rainbow quilt, however, before I found out that my rainbow baby didn't make it. I lost another baby girl at 18 weeks again, all in the same year.

"Although my grief was intense, I decided to finish the quilt and gift it to my sister who was also pregnant at the time,

with her own rainbow baby. This quilt became my therapy. It meant so much to me to be able to finish it and hand it over to her as a gift from my babies to hers. It took me a long time to finish the quilt, but I did and I was able to gift it to her just before she gave birth to her son. It was a really special moment for both of us and she now keeps the quilt hanging in her home.

"At the beginning of 2019, I found out I was finally pregnant again. I was determined to keep my mind occupied during this anxiety-filled pregnancy with some quilting therapy. After sewing up a few receiving blankets, I figured I'd give making another rainbow-colored quilt a shot. I really, really wanted to wrap my newborn baby in one. While searching for some more baby quilt ideas, I came across a Missouri Star tutorial on how to make a rag quilt. I thought it was so cute and simple enough; I could do it without feeling anxious about the results. Happily, I gave birth to my double-rainbow baby boy on September 11, 2019. I couldn't believe I was finally able to wrap my baby in that rainbow-colored blanket and bring him home.

"I know to some people, they just see blankets, but to me, quilts are so much more. There are prayers and hopes and unspoken dreams all sewn into those fabrics and given to others as an expression of warmth and love. Rainbow baby quilts have become a passion for me. I understand deeply what they represent and I am always humbled to give one."

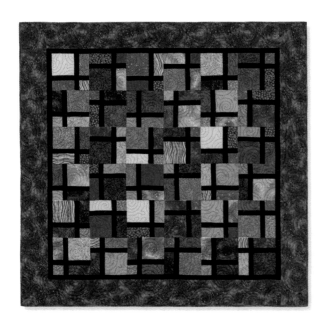

materials

QUILT SIZE
57" x 57"

BLOCK SIZE
15½" unfinished, 15" finished

QUILT TOP
2 packages 5" print squares
1 roll 1½" background strips*
   - includes inner border

OUTER BORDER
1 yard

BINDING
½ yard

BACKING
3¾ yards - vertical seam(s)

*__Note:__ *1 yard of background fabric,*
cut into (21) 1½" width of fabric strips,
can be substituted for the roll of background strips.

SAMPLE QUILT
Laurel Burch Basics Prism Metallic by Gabrielle
Niel Design Studio for Riley Blake Designs

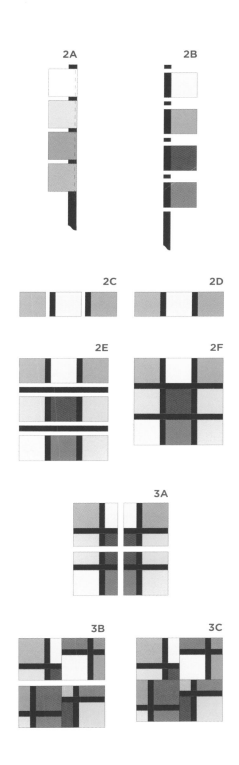

1 cut

From the 1½" background strips:
Select 19 strips and set them aside for another project.* Select 7 strips and set them aside for the 9-patch windowpane sashing. Select 5 strips and set them aside for the inner border.

***Note:** If you chose to cut the strips from yardage, you will not have the extra 19 strips to set aside.

From the remaining (9) 1½" background strips, cut each into (2) 15½" strips for a **total of (18)** 15½" sashing strips.

2 make 9-patch windowpanes

Select (3) 5" print squares and set them aside for another project.

Select (54) 5" squares and the 7 background strips set aside earlier. Use modified chain piecing to quickly sew blocks together. Lay a 5" print square on top of a 1½" background strip, right sides together, lining up the right edges. Sew together using a ¼" seam allowance. Take a few stitches beyond the square. Place another 5" square and sew it to the strip. Continue in this fashion adding up to 8 print squares to each of the 7 background strips. **2A**

Press the seam allowances toward the squares. Trim off the excess fabric between squares. **Make 54** sashed units. **2B**

Sew (1) 5" print square and 2 sashed units together, as shown, making sure each square is a different print fabric. **Make 36** pieced strips. **2C 2D**

Lay out 3 different pieced strips and (2) 15½" sashing strips as shown. Sew the rows together to make a 9-patch windowpane unit. **Make 9. 2E 2F**

3 block construction

Taking 1 of the 9-patch windowpanes, cut the unit in half vertically and horizontally to create 4 quadrants. Cut each of the remaining 9-patch windowpanes in the same manner. **3A**

Tip: Folding the 9-patch windowpane in half and ironing a crease will create a cutting guide line or you can cut 2¼" from the sashing.

Select 4 quadrants from different blocks and lay out your block as shown. Sew the block together in 2 rows. Press the seam of the top row to the right and the seam of the bottom row to the left. Nest the seams and sew the rows together. **Make 9** blocks. **3B 3C**

Block Size: 15½" unfinished, 15" finished

4 arrange & sew

Referring to the diagram on page 69, lay out your blocks in **3 rows** of **3 blocks** each. Sew the blocks together in rows. Press the seam allowances of rows 1 and 3 to the left and row 2 to the right. Nest the seams and sew the rows together.

1 Sew (1) 5" print square and 2 sashed units together, as shown, making sure each square is a different print fabric. Make 36 pieced strips.

2 Lay out 3 different pieced strips and (2) 15½" sashing strips as shown. Sew the rows together to make a 9-patch windowpane unit. Make 9.

3 Taking 1 of the 9-patch windowpanes, cut the unit in half vertically and horizontally to create 4 quadrants. Cut each of the remaining 9-patch windowpanes in the same manner.

4 Select 4 quadrants from different 9-patch windowpanes and lay out your block as shown. Sew the block together in 2 rows. Match the seams and sew the rows together. Make 9 blocks.

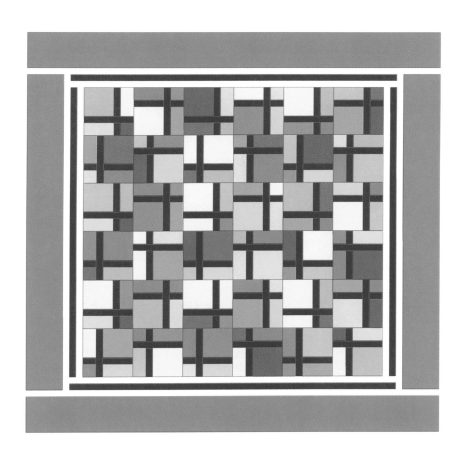

5 inner border

Take (5) 1½" background strips you set aside earlier and sew them end-to-end to make 1 long strip. Trim the borders from this strip.

Refer to Borders (pg. 102) in the Construction Basics to measure and cut the inner borders. The strips are approximately 45½" for the sides and approximately 47½" for the top and bottom.

6 outer border

Cut (6) 5½" strips across the width of the fabric. Sew the strips together end-to-end to make 1 long strip. Trim the borders from this strip.

Refer to Borders (pg. 102) in the Construction Basics to measure and cut the outer borders. The strips are approximately 47½" for the sides and approximately 57½" for the top and bottom.

7 quilt & bind

Layer the quilt with batting and backing and quilt. After the quilting is complete, square up the quilt and trim away all excess batting and backing. Add binding to complete the quilt. See Construction Basics (pg. 102) for binding instructions.

Piece by Piece *by Carole Lowe*
3D Pinwheel Triple Play - Pinwheel Patch

Quilting heals the soul. No matter what trials come my way, it seems I can always put my life back together "piece by piece" through quilting, and I know I'm not the only one. Caroline Beth Townsend shared this sweet story of quilting through the heartache of losing her dear mother, Carol Lowe:

"For many years I was simply a 'quilting dabbler,' but two months before my mother passed away, she tasked me with finishing her UFOs.

"Working on Mom's quilts helped me through the grief process. I felt connected to her as I finished each project, and her passion for quilting was kindled in my own heart. That was five years and close to 100 quilts ago."

The most daunting project was a Hawaiian appliqué quilt Caroline's mother had referred to as her 'lifetime quilt' as it was going to take her a lifetime to finish it. It was meant to have sixteen blocks, all appliquéd and quilted by hand.

Over the course of twenty years, Caroline's mother had completed eight blocks. Another block had been appliquéd but not quilted. The rest were in various stages of appliqué, and the fabrics were stained and damaged with age. Caroline decided to machine quilt that ninth block and finish the quilt with just nine blocks. "Maybe someday I'll go back to those unfinished squares and see if I can revive them, but I'll definitely wait until my skills have improved."

When the quilt was finished, Caroline gave it to her sister, Joan. This is an excerpt of the letter that accompanied that gift:

"... As I have been working on Mom's quilts, this one in particular was the most difficult, not just in skill, but emotionally as well. My stitching looked so terrible next to Mom's that I ripped out my work several times, eventually succumbing to tears.

"I remember Mom telling me about the African violets she inherited when Grandma passed away. Despite her best efforts, the violets slowly died one by one. Mom said she felt that she had disappointed her mother. That's how I felt working on this quilt.

"My husband, in his wisdom and compassion, pointed out that my work wasn't supposed to look like Mom's. After all, these quilts are a joint effort between a mother and daughter, and they represent the love we have for each other and for the quilts' recipients.

"With that realization, and knowing that Mom eventually did learn how to successfully grow African violets, I have been able to continue her projects with joy and the knowledge that, although my skills may never match Mom's, she'll always be inspiring me.

"I want you to have this quilt because it represents Mom's lifetime love for her family and for her craft, which I'm proud to carry on in her honor. That love is forever woven into the threads of this quilt. Think of us both every time you wrap yourselves in its warmth."

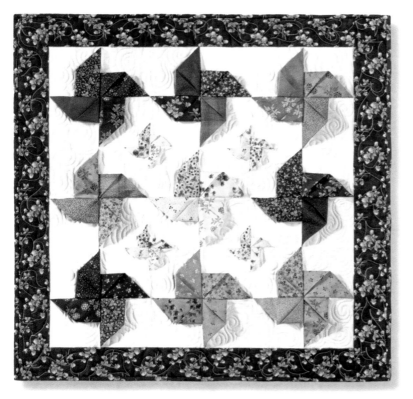

materials

WALL HANGING SIZE
33" x 33"

BLOCK SIZE
9½" unfinished, 9" finished

PROJECT SUPPLIES
1 package 5" print squares
1 package 5" background squares

BORDER
½ yard

BINDING
½ yard

BACKING
1¼ yards

SAMPLE QUILT
Clover Meadow by Jan Patek Quilts for
Moda Fabrics

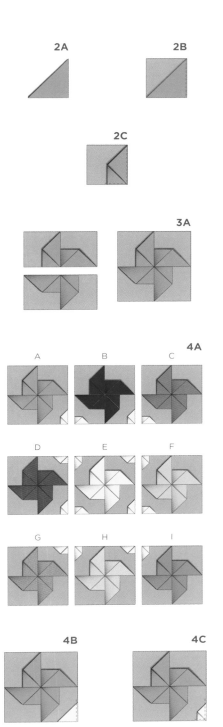

2A 2B

2C

3A

4A

A   B   C

D   E   F

G   H   I

4B 4C

1 sort & cut

Sort your package of 5″ print squares into 10 sets of 4 squares of similar colors. Set the 2 remaining print squares along with (6) 5″ background squares aside for another project.

Choose 1 set of print squares to use for the small pinwheels. Cut each square of your chosen set in half horizontally and vertically to create (4) 2½″ squares for a **total of (16)** 2½″ print squares. Set these aside for the moment.

2 make large pinwheel units

Fold a 5″ print square from corner to corner once on the diagonal with wrong sides together and press the crease in place. **2A** Place the folded piece onto the bottom right corner of a 5″ background square. Align the raw edges of the folded piece with the raw edges of the background square. Baste across the right side using an ⅛″ seam allowance. (We want this seam allowance to be smaller than usual.) **2B**

Fold the loose corner of the folded piece toward the sewn seam on the right. Pin in place. Baste across the bottom of the square using an ⅛″ seam allowance. **2C**

Repeat the steps to fold and baste the remaining matching print squares to background squares to **make 36** units. Keep the units in sets of 4 with similar colors.

3 block construction

Select 1 set of large pinwheel units. Arrange the units as shown. Sew the units together in 2 rows. Press the seam of the top row to the right and the seam of the bottom row to the left. Nest the seams and sew the rows together to complete the block. **Make 9. 3A**

Block Size: 9½″ unfinished, 9″ finished

4 add small pinwheel units

Refer to diagram **4A** to assign your blocks to the positions within the project.

Fold a 2½″ print square from corner to corner once on the diagonal with wrong sides together and press the crease in place. Place the folded piece onto the bottom right corner of Block A. Align the raw edges of the folded piece with the raw edges of the block and baste across the right side using an ⅛″ seam allowance. **4B**

Fold the loose corner of the folded piece toward the sewn seam on the right. Pin in place. Baste across the bottom of the block using an ⅛″ seam allowance. **4C**

Refer back to **4A** for placement of the small pinwheel units. Repeat the steps to fold and baste small pinwheel units in the corners of the blocks.

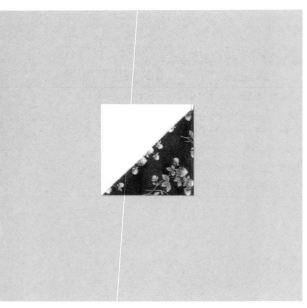

1 Place the folded piece onto the bottom right corner of a 5" background square, as shown. Baste across the right side using an ⅛" seam allowance.

2 Fold the loose corner of the folded piece toward the sewn seam on the right. Pin in place. Baste across the bottom of the square using an ⅛" seam allowance. Make 36 units.

3 Arrange 4 matching pinwheel units as shown. Sew the units together in 2 rows. Match the seams and sew the rows together to complete the block. Make 9.

4 Place the 2½" folded piece onto the bottom right corner of Block A, as shown. Baste across the right side using an ⅛" seam allowance.

5 Fold the loose corner of the folded piece toward the sewn seam on the right. Pin and baste across the bottom of the block using an ⅛" seam allowance.

Units A, C, G, and I each have 1 small pinwheel unit to a corner of the block. Units B, D, F, and H each have 2 small pinwheel units added. Unit E has a small pinwheel unit added to all 4 corners of the block.

5 arrange & sew

Refer to the diagram below as needed to lay out the blocks in **3 rows** with each

row being made up of **3 blocks**. Be sure to pay close attention to the orientation of the blocks so that the small pinwheel units meet to create small pinwheels. Sew the blocks together in rows. Press the seams of the top and bottom rows to the right and the seams of the middle row to the left. Nest the seams and sew the rows together.

6 border

Cut (4) 3½" strips across the width of the fabric. Sew the strips together end-to-end to make 1 long strip. Trim the borders from this strip.

Refer to Borders (pg. 102) in the Construction Basics to measure and cut the borders. The strips are approximately 27½" for the sides and approximately 33½" for the top and bottom.

7 quilt & bind

Layer the wall hanging with batting and backing and quilt. **Note:** You will want to be sure to quilt around the pinwheels so that they remain 3-dimensional.

After the quilting is complete, square up the wall hanging and trim away all excess batting and backing.

Add binding to complete the wall hanging. See Construction Basics (pg. 102) for binding instructions.

Pinwheel Dance

materials

PROJECT SIZE
Fits a 20" pillow

BLOCK SIZE
9½" unfinished, 9" finished

PROJECT SUPPLIES
(8) 5" print squares
1½ yards background fabric
   - includes pillow back
22½" square of batting

OPTIONAL PILLOW INSERT
¾ yard muslin
Fiberfill

Don't have a pillow form handy?

Simply cut (2) 17" squares of fabric and sew them together around the perimeter using a ½" seam allowance with right sides facing. Leave an opening about 4-6" wide for turning. Clip the corners and turn right side out. Stuff the pillow with fiberfill and whipstitch the opening closed.

1 cut

Cut each 5″ print square in half horizontally and vertically to create (4) 2½″ squares from each. Set these aside for the moment, keeping matching squares together.

From the background fabric, cut:

- (2) 3″ strips across the width of the fabric. Subcut the strips into (28) 3″ squares.

- (1) 14″ strip across the width of the fabric. Subcut (2) 14″ x 21″ rectangles. Set these aside for the pillow back.

- (1) 24½″ strip across the width of the fabric. Subcut a 24½″ square for the pillow top backing.

From the remaining 24½″ piece of background fabric, cut:

- (1) 3″ strip across the width of the fabric. Subcut into (4) 3″ squares. Add these to the 3″ squares cut previously for a **total of (32)** 3″ squares.

- (2) 5½″ strips across the width of the fabric. Subcut 1 strip into (1) 5½″ square and (3) 5½″ x 3″ rectangles. Subcut the second strip into (5) 5½″ x 3″ rectangles.

- (1) 8″ strip across the width of the fabric. Subcut (4) 8″ x 3″ rectangles.

2 make pinwheel blocks

Pick up a set of matching 2½″ print squares. Fold each print square from

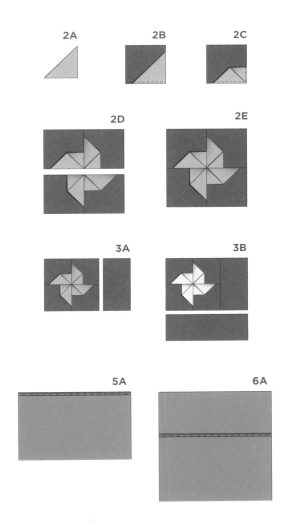

corner to corner once on the diagonal with wrong sides together and press the crease in place. **2A**

Place 1 folded piece onto the bottom right corner of a 3″ background square. Align the raw edges of the folded piece with the raw edges of the background square. Baste across the bottom of the square using an ⅛″ seam allowance. (We want this seam allowance to be smaller than usual.) **2B**

Fold the loose corner of the folded piece toward the sewn seam on the bottom. Pin in place. Baste the right side of the square using an ⅛" seam allowance. Repeat the steps to fold and sew the remaining print squares to 3" background squares to **make 4** matching quadrants. **2C**

Lay out 4 matching quadrants as shown. Using a ¼" seam allowance, sew the quadrants together in 2 rows. Press the seam of the top row to the right and the seam of the bottom row to the left. Nest the seams and sew the rows together to complete the block. **Make 8**. **2D 2E**

Block Size: 5" finished

3 arrange & sew

Sew a 5½" x 3" background rectangle on the right side of each block to **make 8** A Units. **3A**

Refer to the diagram to the right and assign your blocks to the positions within the pillow top. Sew an 8" x 3" background rectangle to the bottom of the 4 blocks assigned as B Units. **3B**

Referring to the diagram to the right, lay your pillow top out in 3 rows paying attention to the orientation of each block. Sew a B Unit to both sides of an A Unit for the top and bottom rows. Sew an A Unit to both sides of the 5½" background square for the middle row.

Press the seams of the top and bottom row to the right and the seams of the middle row

to the left. Nest the seams and sew the rows together to complete the pillow top.

4 quilt the pillow top

Layer your pillow top on top of the batting and backing square. Baste and quilt using your favorite methods. **Note:** Be sure to quilt around the pinwheels so that they remain 3-dimensional.

After the quilting is complete, square up and trim away all excess batting and backing.

5 make the pillow back

Fold a long edge of a 14" x 21" rectangle over ½" with wrong sides touching. Press. Repeat a second time to enclose the raw

edge of the fabric. Topstitch along the folded edge. Repeat to finish 1 long edge of the remaining rectangle to create the 2 pillow back flaps. **5A**

6 finish the pillow

Lay the pillow top with the right side facing up. Lay the 2 pillow back flaps on top, with the right sides facing down, making sure that the pillow back flaps overlap each other by about 4". **6A**

Pin or clip the pillow back flaps to the pillow top. Sew around the perimeter of the pillow using a ½" seam allowance. Finish the edges with a serger or zigzag stitch to prevent fraying.

Clip the corners and turn the pillow right sides out. Insert a pillow form to finish your project.

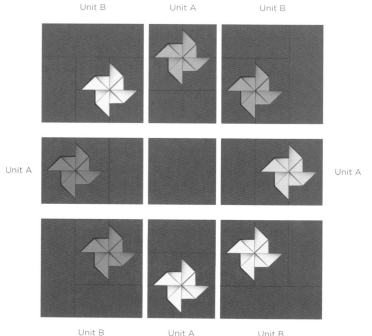

Pinwheel Toss

materials

TABLE RUNNER SIZE
49½" x 13½"

BLOCK SIZE
14" unfinished, 13½" finished

TABLE RUNNER SUPPLIES
1 package 5" print squares
½ yard white solid fabric

BINDING
½ yard

BACKING
1 yard - cut parallel to the selvages
   and sewn together along the
   short ends

2A

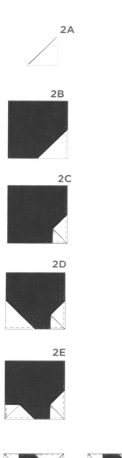

2B

2C

2D

2E

2F

1 cut & sort

From the white solid fabric, cut:

- (2) 2½" strips across the width of the fabric. Subcut (16) 2½" squares from each strip for a **total of (32)** 2½" white squares.
- (2) 1¾" strips across the width of the fabric. Subcut (1) 1¾" x 23" rectangle from each strip.

Set the remaining white solid fabric aside for another project. Set the rectangles aside for the moment.

Select 18 dark print squares and 13 light print squares from your package of 5" squares. Set the remaining print squares aside for another project. Choose 3 of your selected light print squares and cut them in half lengthwise creating |(2) 2½" x 5" rectangles from each square. You will need a **total of 5** light print rectangles. Set the rectangles and remaining light print squares aside for the moment.

2 make pinwheel units

Fold each 2½" white square from corner to corner once on the diagonal with wrong sides together and press the crease in place. **2A**

Unit A

Place a folded piece onto the bottom right corner of a 5" dark print square. Align the raw edges of the folded piece with the raw edges of the print square. Baste across the right side using an ⅛" seam allowance. (We want this seam allowance to be smaller than usual.) **2B**

Fold the loose corner of the folded piece toward the sewn seam on the right. Pin in place. Baste across the bottom of the square using an ⅛" seam allowance. Repeat the steps to baste the remaining folded pieces to dark print squares. **Make 18. 2C**

Unit B

To make a Unit B, place a folded piece onto the bottom left corner of a Unit A. Align the raw edges of the folded piece with the raw edges of the dark print square and baste across the bottom using an ⅛" seam allowance. **2D**

Fold the loose corner of the folded piece toward the sewn seam on the bottom. Pin in place. Baste across the left side of the unit using an ⅛" seam allowance. Repeat the steps to baste folded pieces to the units. **Make 10. 2E**

Unit C

To make the Unit C, select a Unit B. Follow the previous steps to baste folded pieces to the 2 remaining corners. **Make 2. 2F**

3 make pinwheel blocks

Lay out the units in 3 rows of 3 units as shown in diagram **3A**. Be sure to pay close attention to the orientation of the units. The top row and bottom row will consist of a Unit A, a Unit B, and a Unit A in that order. The middle row will consist of a Unit B, a Unit C, and another Unit B in that order. Using a ¼" seam allowance, sew the units together in 3 rows. Press the seams of the top and bottom rows to the right and the seams of the middle

3A

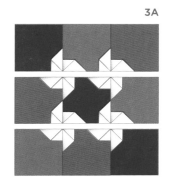

4A

4B

4C

row to the left. Nest the seams and sew the rows together to complete the block. **Make 2.**

Block Size: 14″ unfinished, 13½″ finished

4 make stripes

Sew (5) 5″ light print squares side-by-side to form a wide stripe. **Make 2** wide stripes. **4A**

Take the (5) 2½″ x 5″ light print rectangles and sew them end-to-end to create the center stripe. **4B**

Sew a 1¾″ x 23″ white rectangle to the top and bottom of the center stripe to create a center unit. **4C**

Sew a wide stripe to the top and bottom of the center unit to complete the stripe unit. **4D**

5 arrange & sew

Lay out the table runner as shown in the diagram below. Sew a pinwheel block to either end of the stripe unit.

6 quilt & bind

Layer the table runner with batting and backing and quilt. **Note:** Be sure to quilt around the pinwheels so that they remain 3-dimensional.

After the quilting is complete, square up the table runner and trim away all excess batting and backing. Add binding to complete the table runner. See Construction Basics (pg. 102) for binding instructions.

4D

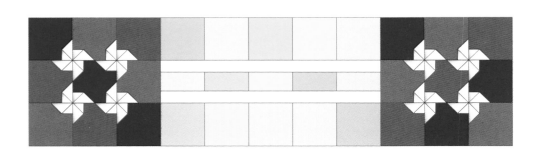

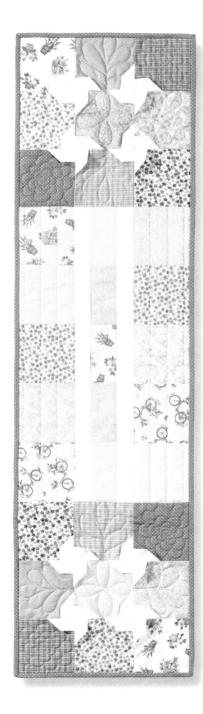

Bernie shook her head. "I'm sorry. I couldn't."

"If you know something, it could help Blair a lot. And this is all happening at Gina's request," Jenny said.

"Well, both Gina and Rachel are gone now, so I suppose it's all right." Bernie swallowed and looked between them still nervous. "I went to visit Rachel one day. She was in tears. Sobbing. No one else was there, and Rachel told me that Gina—Gina was pregnant."

"You're kidding me," Dotty hissed, keeping her eyes on Bernie as she soaked in a secret that had long been kept from her.

Bernie's voice dropped almost to a whisper, as if she still couldn't believe she was telling the secret. "Gina didn't tell her 'till the middle of summer. The baby would have been due at the beginning of the new school year and Rachel didn't know what to do. She was so afraid Gina's life would be ruined."

"And Rachel just told you?" Jenny asked. "That's kind of surprising. It would have been quite a scandal."

Bernie shrugged, the sadness weighing her down until her shoulders drooped. "I was a friend, and I caught her at the right moment. Or maybe it was the wrong moment. I'm not sure."

"You already knew Gina's secret." The words were muffled behind Dotty's hand.

Bernie nodded, her voice heavy as she relived the conversations. "I didn't think anyone else was supposed to know. Rachel sent Gina away to stay with her grandmother or something like that. And we didn't bring it up."

Jenny tapped the table, still trying to put the puzzle pieces together. "But you said Rachel talked about it more than once."

"Well, yes. When I heard Gina was coming home, I asked her what happened with the baby. She brushed it off like it was no big deal. Said it was handled. The baby was gone and Gina wouldn't be ruined after all."

"But what happened?" Jenny leaned toward Bernie. She'd been so close to learning the truth and now she only had more questions.

Bernie shrugged. "I don't know. The baby was just gone. It may have not made it. Gina never did gain much weight during the time I saw her. Maybe the baby was given up for adoption."

"Is there anyone else Rachel might have talked to?" Jenny asked.

"Not likely." Bernie's face was drawn.

"What about friends? Is there anyone else still in town from Gina's high school years?" Jenny kept hoping Bernie had something more to add.

"You could ask Claudia. They knew each other pretty well." Bernie looked to Dotty. "Are you ready to go? I'm kind of tired."

Jenny could have sworn Claudia said she and Gina had not been friends but she didn't push it.

Bernie and Dotty left, leaving Jenny to stew over the new information. She stepped outside and leaned over the railing, hoping she could tell if Ron had finished fixing the door.

Across the grassy lawn from Jenny's studio, she could see Sam's food truck parked in the alley for the night. A light moved inside, and a crash rang out.

"Did you hear that?" Jenny asked, not taking her eyes off the dark shadow of the truck.

There was no answer from Ron.

"You're almost done, right?" she called louder.

A trickle of nerves started working its way into her chest, but after a clunk of metal, he responded, "Almost!"

Jenny let her relief settle before she hurried down the steps. She wanted to make sure everything was alright with the Peters' food truck before she and Ron left.

"I'll be right back," she called, and made her way across the street.

The street light didn't do much to illuminate the space behind the food truck, but it looked empty.

A door slammed at the back of the vehicle.

"Sam?" she called, hoping he was the one staying late.

No one answered. The hairs on the back of her neck rose. She peeked around the back end of the vehicle. Why hadn't she waited for Ron?

A set of keys was splayed on the ground next to the rear door. Jenny bent to pick them up. In that same moment, the door swung open.

She screamed, and someone scrambled down the steps with a large, fat envelope in his hand. He grabbed her, spinning her toward the door, and clamped his hand down on her shoulder. Her attacker shoved his knee into her back, pushing her down into the steps.

"You shouldn't be here." His gravelly voice grated in her ear.

"Who are you?"

He didn't answer, only pushed down harder, leaning around her like he was looking for something. She closed her fist around the keys and the man pulled her up, pinning her against the door. She couldn't turn around, couldn't see anything.

He wrenched her hand out from behind her back, the paper envelope cutting her bare skin as he pulled the keys from her grip.

Then, someone tore around the corner of the vehicle followed by the sound of a thud, and her attacker let go.

Ron wrapped Jenny in his arms as the man quickly escaped. Footsteps echoed down the alley.

"He's getting away!" Jenny panicked, pulling back from her husband's embrace.

"It's okay. We'll call the police."

"It's not okay. We have to stop him!" Jenny put a hand to her head. The footsteps pounding like a headache.

Ron pulled out his cellphone, dialed the police, and held Jenny closer while it rang.

With a little sob, she leaned into her husband. "What just happened?"

Ron's hand brushed up the back of her neck and her shoulders started to shake. He answered, "Yes? Officer Wilkins? Thanks for taking my call. I need to report an attack."

to be continued...

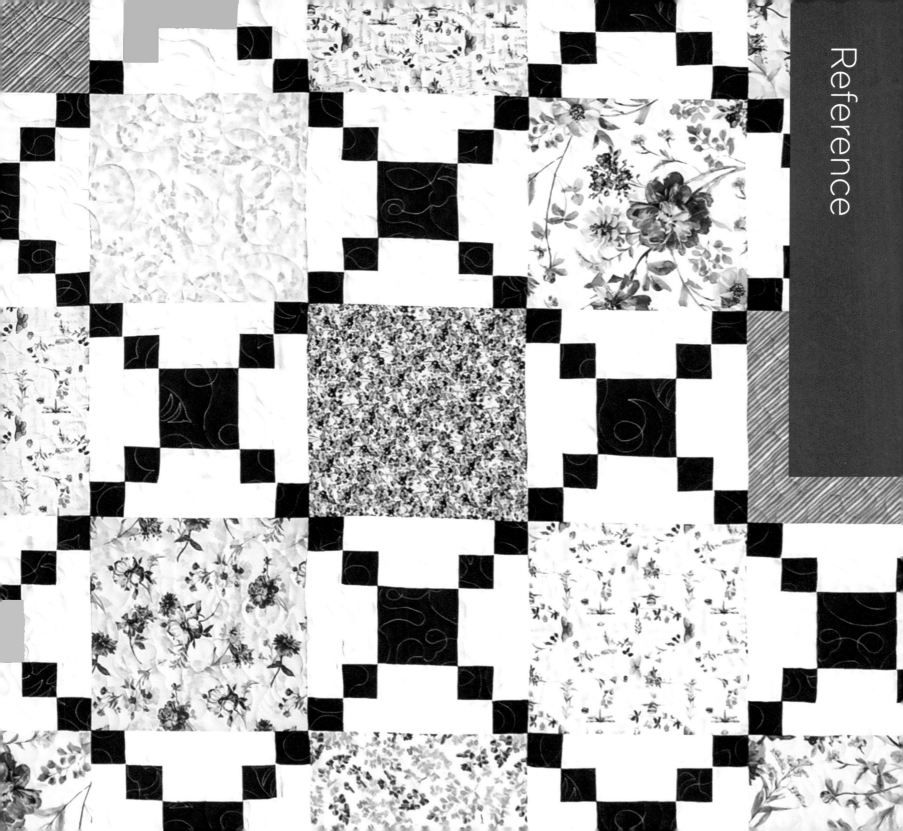

Pinwheel Toss

TABLE RUNNER SIZE
49½" x 13½"

BLOCK SIZE
14" unfinished, 13½" finished

TABLE RUNNER SUPPLIES
1 package 5" print squares
½ yard white solid fabric

BINDING
½ yard

BACKING
1 yard - cut parallel to the selvages
   and sewn together along the
   short ends

SAMPLE QUILT
Butterfly Garden by Cheryl Haynes
for Benartex

QUILTING PATTERN
Custom quilted by Janet Yamamoto

PATTERN
P. 82

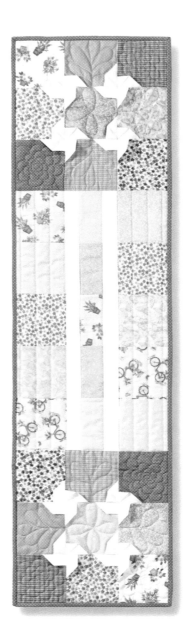

Pinwheel Dance

PILLOW SIZE
Fits a 20" pillow

BLOCK SIZE
9½" unfinished, 9" finished

PROJECT SIZE
(8) 5" print squares
1½ yards background fabric
  - includes pillow back
22½" square of batting

OPTIONAL PILLOW INSERT
¾ yard muslin
Fiberfill

SAMPLE PILLOW
Tonga Treats Batiks by Timeless Treasures

QUILTING PATTERN
Custom quilted by Janet Yamamoto

PATTERN
P. 78

Pinwheel
Patch

WALL HANGING SIZE
33" x 33"

BLOCK SIZE
9½" unfinished, 9" finished

PROJECT SUPPLIES
1 package 5" print squares
1 package 5" background squares

BORDER
½ yard

BINDING
½ yard

BACKING
1¼ yards

SAMPLE QUILT
Clover Meadow by Jan Patek Quilts for
Moda Fabrics

QUILT PATTERN
Custom quilted by Natalie Earnheart

PAGE
P. 72

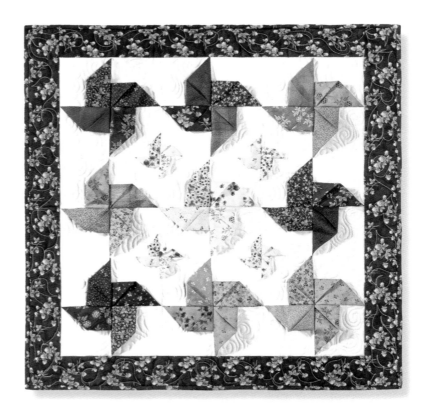

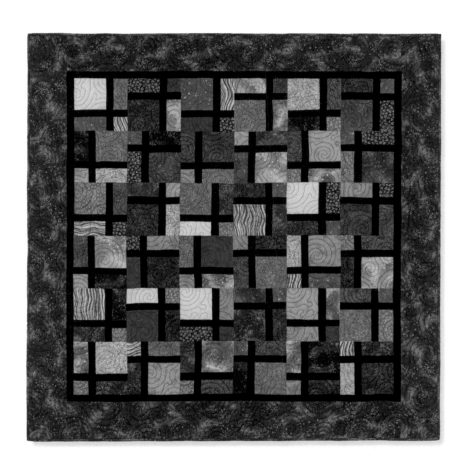

Disappearing 9-Patch Windowpane

QUILT SIZE
57" x 57"

BLOCK SIZE
15½" unfinished, 15" finished

QUILT TOP
2 packages 5" print squares
1 roll 1½" background strips*
 - includes inner border

OUTER BORDER
1 yard

BINDING
½ yard

BACKING
3¾ yards - vertical seam(s)

__Note:__ 1 yard of background fabric, cut into (21) 1½" width of fabric strips, can be substituted for the roll of background strips.

SAMPLE QUILT
Laurel Burch Basics Prism Metallic
by Gabrielle Niel Design Studio for Riley Blake Designs

QUILTING PATTERN
Sticky Buns

PATTERN
P. 66

Irish Change

QUILT SIZE
100½" x 100½"

BLOCK SIZE
10" unfinished, 9½" finished

QUILT TOP
1 package 10" print squares
1½ yards accent fabric
3¼ yards background fabric
 – includes inner border

OUTER BORDER
1¾ yards

BINDING
1 yard

BACKING
9¼ yards – vertical seam(s)
 or 3¼ yards 108" wide

SAMPLE QUILT
Sketchbook Garden by Lisa Audit
for Wilmington Prints
Bella Solids - American Blue by
Moda Fabrics

QUILTING PATTERN
Buzzing Around

PAGE
P. 16

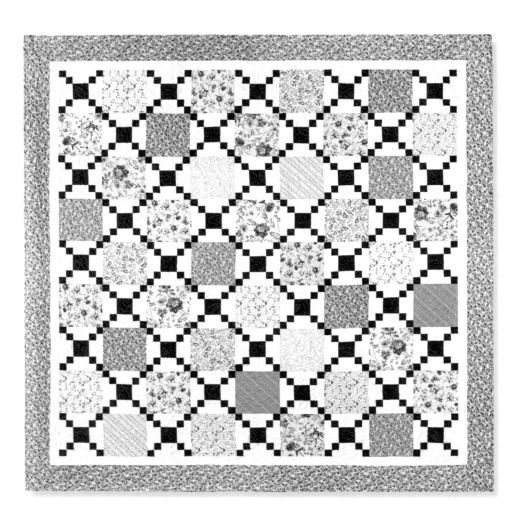

Luminary

QUILT SIZE
58" x 72"

BLOCK SIZE
12½" unfinished, 12" finished

QUILT TOP
3 packages 5" print squares
  - includes cornerstones
3¾ yards background fabric
  - includes sashing

BINDING
¾ yard

BACKING
3¾ yards - horizontal seam(s)

SAMPLE QUILT
Good Times by American Jane for
Moda Fabrics

QUILTING PATTERN
Free Swirls

PATTERN
P. 24

Road Trip

QUILT SIZE
72″ x 81½″

BLOCK SIZE
10″ unfinished, 9½″ finished

QUILT TOP
1 package 10″ print squares
1 package 10″ background squares

INNER BORDER
¾ yard

OUTER BORDER
1½ yards

BINDING
¾ yard

BACKING
5 yards - vertical seam(s)
    or 2½ yards 108″ wide

OTHER
2¾ yards Heat n Bond Lite

SAMPLE QUILT
Fiddle Dee Dee by Me & My Sister
Designs for Moda Fabrics

QUILTING PATTERN
Carstory

PAGE
P. 54

Road Trip Pillow

PROJECT SIZE
Fits a 16" pillow form

BLOCK SIZE
12" unfinished, 11½" finished

PROJECT SUPPLIES
(16) 2½" print squares
½ yard coordinating fabric
 - includes borders and pillow back
½ yard background fabric

OTHER
8½" square of Heat n Bond Lite
17" square of batting

OPTIONAL PILLOW INSERT
½ yard muslin
Fiberfill

SAMPLE QUILT
Fiddle Dee Dee by Me & My Sister
Designs for Moda Fabrics

QUILTING PATTERN
Free motion quilted
by Carol Henderson

PATTERN
P. 60

Ruby Sensation
Sew-Along

QUILT SIZE
86" x 86"

QUILT TOP
1¼ yards fabric A
1¼ yards fabric B
1½ yards fabric C
1¼ yards fabric D
5½ yards background fabric
  - includes inner border

OUTER BORDER
1½ yards

BINDING
¾ yard

BACKING
6¼ yards – vertical seam(s)
  or 2½ yards 108" wide

SAMPLE QUILT
Kona Solids Crimson, Chinese Red,
Tomato, Sienna, White

Missouri Star

BLOCK SIZE
24½" unfinished, 24" finished

BLOCK ONLY
¼ yard fabric A or (1) 10" square
¼ yard fabric B or (2) 10" squares
¼ yard fabric C or (2) 10" squares
1 yard background fabric
  or (9) 10" squares

QUILTING PATTERN
Meander

PAGE
P. 12

Stars & Stitches

QUILT SIZE
55" x 55"

BLOCK SIZE
16½" unfinished, 16" finished

QUILT TOP
1 package 10" print squares

SASHING & BORDER
1 yard

BINDING
½ yard

BACKING
3½ yards

OTHER
Creative Grids® Crazier
   Eight Template Set

SAMPLE QUILT
Esther's Heirloom Shirtings by
Kim Diehl for Henry Glass

QUILTING PATTERN
Champagne Bubbles

PATTERN
P. 34

Wonder by
Katie Larson

QUILT SIZE
72″ x 72″

BLOCK SIZE
36½″ unfinished, 36″ finished

QUILT TOP
½ yard - navy fabric
¾ yard - light blue, red, yellow, light
  gray, and dark gray fabrics
1¼ yards - purple, teal, cream,
  and pink fabrics

BINDING
¾ yard

BACKING
4½ yards - vertical seam(s)
  or 2¼ yards of 108″ wide

SAMPLE QUILT
Solid fabrics from various
manufacturers

QUILTING PATTERN
Custom quilted by Katie Larson

PATTERN
P. 44

Wonder Variation

QUILT SIZE
72″ x 72″

BLOCK SIZE
36½″ unfinished, 36″ finished

QUILT TOP
½ yard - FBY-81445
¾ yard - FBY-81446, FBY-81444,
    FBY-81455, FBY-81453, Background
1¼ yards - FBY-81457, FBY-81450,
    FBY-81447, FBY-81452

BINDING
¾ yard

BACKING
4½ yards - vertical seam(s)
    or 2¼ yards of 108″ wide

SAMPLE QUILT
Desert Sun by Kathy Engle
for Island Batik

PATTERN
Aztec

PAGE
P. 44

Construction Basics

General Quilting

- All seams are ¼" inch unless directions specify differently.
- Cutting instructions are given at the point when cutting is required.
- Precuts are not prewashed; therefore do not prewash other fabrics in the project.
- All strips are cut width of fabric.
- Remove all selvages.

Press Seams

- Use a steam iron on the cotton setting.
- Press the seam just as it was sewn right sides together. This "sets" the seam.
- With dark fabric on top, lift the dark fabric and press back.
- The seam allowance is pressed toward the dark side. Some patterns may direct otherwise for certain situations.
- Follow pressing arrows in the diagrams when indicated.
- Press toward borders. Pieced borders may demand otherwise.
- Press diagonal seams open on binding to reduce bulk.

Borders

- Always measure the quilt top 3 times before cutting borders.
- Start measuring about 4" in from each side and through the center vertically.
- Take the average of those 3 measurements.
- Cut 2 border strips to that size. Piece strips together if needed.
- Attach 1 to either side of the quilt.

- Position the border fabric on top as you sew. The feed dogs can act like rufflers. Having the border on top will prevent waviness and keep the quilt straight.
- Repeat this process for the top and bottom borders, measuring the width 3 times.
- Include the newly attached side borders in your measurements.
- Press toward the borders.

Binding

find a video tutorial at: www.msqc.co/006

- Use 2½" strips for binding.
- Sew strips end-to-end into 1 long strip with diagonal seams, aka the plus sign method (next). Press seams open.
- Fold in half lengthwise wrong sides together and press.
- The entire length should equal the outside dimension of the quilt plus 15" - 20."

Plus Sign Method

- Lay 1 strip across the other as if to make a plus sign right sides together.
- Sew from top inside to bottom outside corners crossing the intersections of fabric as you sew.
  Trim excess to ¼" seam allowance.
- Press seam open.

find a video tutorial at: www.msqc.co/001

Attach Binding

- Match raw edges of folded binding to the quilt top edge.
- Leave a 10" tail at the beginning.
- Use a ¼" seam allowance.
- Start in the middle of a long straight side.

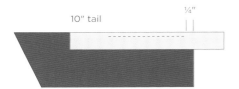

10" tail   ¼"

Miter Corners

- Stop sewing ¼" before the corner.
- Move the quilt out from under the presser foot.
- Clip the threads.
- Flip the binding up at a 90° angle to the edge just sewn.
- Fold the binding down along the next side to be sewn, aligning raw edges.
- The fold will lie along the edge just completed.
- Begin sewing on the fold.

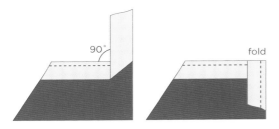

90°   fold

Close Binding

MSQC recommends The Binding Tool from TQM Products to finish binding perfectly every time.

- Stop sewing when you have 12" left to reach the start.
- Where the binding tails come together, trim excess leaving only 2½" of overlap.
- It helps to pin or clip the quilt together at the 2 points where the binding starts and stops. This takes the pressure off of the binding tails while you work.
- Use the plus sign method to sew the 2 binding ends together, except this time when making the plus sign, match the edges. Using a pencil, mark your sewing line because you won't be able to see where the corners intersect. Sew across.

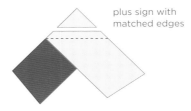

plus sign with matched edges

- Trim off excess; press seam open.
- Fold in half wrong sides together, and align all raw edges to the quilt top.
- Sew this last binding section to the quilt. Press.
- Turn the folded edge of the binding around to the back of the quilt and tack into place with an invisible stitch or machine stitch if you wish.